"Frank and Gordon MacKay, brothers to the bone, have produced a marvelous book that accomplishes what I once thought was impossible...a baseball collection of statistics that's impossible to put down. It's a fitting tribute to their late father, Joe MacKay, that envelopes the spirit of their great diner breakfasts and allows us all to bathe in the deep history of America's great game. It's also a must for every bar in America. It'll resolve conflicts before they get violent. Frank and Gordon have put their love of the game and put flesh and blood into numbers."

Michael Blowen
Former Movie Critic
Founder of Old Friends Equine
Boston Globe

"Frank and Gordon MacKay knock the cover off the horsehide with these intriguing nuggets of baseball's storied record history from the last time a team hit .300 for the season (Boston 1950) to an ignoble list of pitchers who lost, not won, 20 games in a season. A must for any baseball stat junkie."

Rick Brand
Political reporter and columnist
Newsday

The Love of the Game
The Numbers behind our National Pastime

By Frank MacKay, Gordon MacKay and Joe MacKay

Joe MacKay

FOREWORD

Our father and lifelong baseball fan, Joe MacKay, deserves the lion share of the credit for the tireless research that went into creating this book. Before his passing in 2005, he spent a lifetime studying and documenting everything about baseball. He was an author, mathematician, teacher and father who imparted to us an equal love for the game.

Our father loved all kinds of trivia, and throughout the years, he documented offbeat statistics about baseball, which he eagerly shared during our ritual Saturday morning breakfasts at the local diner and over holiday dinners. His love for stats and trivia were infectious and became a game in itself. Over the years, we delved into our own research, seeking to uncover trivia that we knew would have made his day. The result is a book that not only incorporates our collective research, but also our father's love for preserving the historical facts associated with the sport he loved.

As in many American families, baseball to us was a family affair. Our summers were spent traveling to cities with great ballparks. We visited many throughout the United States, and of course made regular trips to Cooperstown, New York like so many other baseball junkies. But unlike most people, our father's intensity about the game was equaled by a love for math and an uncanny memory for people and their historical feats. Without the aid of the internet, he derived his information by utilizing local libraries, and by delving into books and scholarly articles and of course, during those trips to the Baseball Hall of Fame in Cooperstown.

He was a proud member of the Society for American Baseball Research (SABR), and a pioneer in SABR-metrics. Most average baseball fans might have thought his book, <u>Great Shutout Pitchers: Twenty Profiles of a Vanishing Breed</u>, was a little on the dry side. But those who have a passion for baseball facts know that the book was painstakingly researched. It reveals a lot about the sport, but also a lot about the author: he loved facts and the quest for knowledge as much as he loved the game.

With his untimely passing in March 2005, a good body of his research remained incomplete. We felt it was our obligation to continue his quest and finish where he left off. While the official cause of his death was cardiac arrest, we sometimes half-heartedly joke that the Yankees' playoff collapse in 2004 was the fatal blow that eventually did him in. If there is baseball in heaven, we're sure he has season tickets to Yankee Stadium.

This book is dedicated to him, and to all baseball enthusiasts, past and present, who share in the spirit of the game, and revel in the little details that all add up to this great American sport.

- Frank and Gordon MacKay, May 2013

The 700 Club

Since 1900, which is the arbitrary date that modern baseball began, there have been only ten teams that have reached the 700 Club. Note that the Chicago Cubs is the only team to achieve it in consecutive seasons:

American League		National League	
1927 New York	.714	1902 Pittsburgh	.741
1931 Philadelphia	.704	1906 Chicago	.763
1939 New York	.703	1907 Chicago	.704
1954 Cleveland	.721	1909 Pittsburgh	.724
1998 New York	.704		
2001 Seattle	.716		

Teams with 100 Wins in 3 Consecutive Years

Only four times in baseball's history has a team won one hundred games in three consecutive years. Three other times, a team came close to duplicating that feat. Those teams fell one victory short during that stretch. The Chicago Cubs, from 1906 -1910 had four 100-win years. Only the great penna nt race of 1908 broke the string. One can only imagine the disputed game of September 4, 1904, which Brown lost to Willis 1-0. How impressive a consecutive streak of five straight years would have been?

Another close call was the streak the New York Yankees had from 1936 through 1939. In 1938, the Bombers had ninety-nine victories but due to two rainouts that were never made up, they fell short of the century mark. If allowed to make up those games, in all probability, they would have won at least one: but as we all know--baseball is made up of numerous *might have beens*.

Philadelphia A's	St. Louis Cardinals
1929 104-46	1942 106-48
1930 102-52	1943 105-49
1931 107-45	1944 105-49

Baltic Orioles	Atlantic Braves
1969 109-53	1997 101-61

1970 108-54	1998 106-56
1971 101-57	1999 103-59

Close Calls

New York Yankees	Chicago Cubs	Oakland A's
1936 102-51	1906 116-36	1988 104-58
1937 102-52	1907 107-45	1989 99-63
1938 99-53	1908 99-55	1990 103-59
1939 106-45	1909 104-49	
	1910 104-50	

Teams with 100 Wins but No Pennants

When a team wins one hundred games in a season, people assume they should win a pennant. Before the first expansion (1961-1968) there were only four teams that reached the century mark, but failed to win the pennant.

During the first expansion, two teams hit the 100 mark and failed to seize the flag. The 1962 Los Angeles Dodgers lost out in a three game playoff to the San Francisco Giants.

Since divisional play started in 1969, it is not uncommon that teams with 100 or more wins do not necessarily make it to the World Series. Such is the case of the Seattle Mariners in 2001; when they tied the all-time win mark of 116.

American League		National League	
1915 Detroit	100-54	1909 Chicago	104-49
1954 New York	103-51	1942 Brooklyn	104-50

During First Expansion

1961 Detroit	101-61	1962 Los Angeles	102-63

Start of Divisional Play

1971 Oakland	101-60	1976 Philadelphia	101-61
1977 Kansas City	102-60	1977 Philadelphia	101-61
1980 New York	103-59	1998 Atlanta	106-56
1980 Baltimore	100-62	1998 Houston	102-60
2001 Seattle	116-46	1999 Arizona	100-62
2001 Oakland	102-60	2002 Atlanta	101-60
2002 New York	103-58	2003 Atlanta	101-61
2002 Oakland	103-59	2003 San Francisco	100-61

Only Teams to Lead in Hitting, Pitching and Fielding the Same Year

There were only nine teams in baseball's history that led in hitting, pitching and fielding during the same year. Those teams went on to win the pennant seven times. Only Cleveland, in 1906, finished third and Seattle, in 2001, finished first in their division, but lost in the ALCS.

Listed below are the teams:

American League	BA	P (ERA)	Fielding
1906 Cleveland	.279	2.09	.967
1910 Philadelphia	.266	1.79	.965
1948 Cleveland	.282	3.23	.982
2001 Seattle	.288	3.54	.986
National League			
1904 New York	.262	2.18	.956
1906 Chicago	.262	1.76	.969
1944 St. Louis	.275	2.68	.982
1945 Chicago	.277	2.98	.980
1946 St. Louis	.265	3.01	.980

Note that in 1931, National League New York led in pitching but came in second in batting and fielding.

6

<u>Batting</u>		<u>Fielding</u>	
Chicago	.2894	St. Louis	.9737
New York	.2892	New York	.9935

Last Place Clubs Leading in Batting, Pitching and Fielding

It is not often that a cellar dweller can have something to crow about, but on seven occasions, they did lead the league in batting twice, pitching once and fielding four times.

Batting	Pitching	Fielding
National League	National League	American League
1999 Colorado .288	1984 Pittsburgh 3.12	1970 Washington .982
2001 Colorado .292		1924 Boston .973
		1997 Kansas City .985
		1925 Chicago .969

*In 1958, first place Milwaukee hit .2656, while Philadelphia hit .2655

Teams That Hit 300 or More during the Season

A three hundred batting average was achieved forty times in the game's history. It is not just a coincidence that it all happened, except for one year, during the 1920's and 1930's. This was the beginning of the lively ball era, which brought forth the most famous power hitters in the games' annals.

Looking over the stats for those decades, we can see why the year 1930 was called the year of the big boom. This was the year that Hack Wilson had his record 191 RBI's along with fifty-six homers. Bill Terry and Chuck Klein both tallied 250 or more hits. More pronounced was that nine of the sixteen teams batted .300 or better.

When the Boston Red Sox hit .302 in 1950, it was the first time since 1936 this occurred. Little did anyone realize that it would be the last time.

In scanning the following charts, you will note that the Detroit Tigers and the Pittsburgh Pirates led the list with six years each. The Pirates set a record when they hit .300 in four consecutive years.

In looking over the list, you can see that hitting .300 did not ensure a pennant. Only twelve out of the forty times did a pennant winner achieve that number.

American League

Boston	Cleveland	Detroit
1936 .304	1920 .302 (1)	1921 .316
1950 .302	1921 .308	1922 .306
	1923 .301	1923 .300
	1930 .304	1925 .302
		1934 .300 (1)
		1936 .300

New York	Philadelphia	St. Louis	Washington
1921 .300 (1)	1925 .307	1920 .308	1925 .301 (1)
1927 .307 (1)	1927 .303	1921 .304	1930 .302
1930 .309		1922 .313	
1936 .300 (1)			

National League

Brooklyn	Chicago	New York
1930 .304	1929 .303 (1)	1922 .305 (1)
	1930 .309	1924 .307 (1)
		1930 .319

Philadelphia	Pittsburgh	St. Louis
1929 .309	1922 .308	1921 .308
1930 .315	1925 .307 (1)	1922 .301
	1927 .305 (1)	1930 .314 (1)
	1928 .308	
	1929 .303	
	1930 .303	

One Thousand Run Teams

In 2003, everyone was raving about the powerhouse Boston Red Sox and their 961 runs scored. In fact, that total was topped three times recently. In 1998, the New York Yankees scored 965 runs and two teams in 2000 surpassed that mark – the Chicago Whites Sox 978 and Colorado Rockies 968.

Teams that totaled over 1,000 runs in a season dwarf these totals. Six of them did it during 154 game schedules.

American League	*National League*
1930 New York 1062	1930 St. Louis 1004
1931 New York 1067	
1932 New York 1002 (1)	
1936 New York 1065 (1)	
1950 Boston 1027	
1999 Cleveland 1009	

*Chicago in 1930 scored 998 runs

Power up the Middle

The power hitters in a baseball line do not usually include the middle infielders, although in recent years we have seen a surge of power stats emerging. Jeff Kent, Brett Boone and Alfonso Soriano represent power hitters at second base. Shortstops such as Alex Rodriguez, Miguel Tejada and Rich Aurila are among the league's top run producers.

In 1934, the Detroit Tigers had the first double-play combination to tally 100 RBI's each. In 1940, the Boston Red Sox produced a duo in the middle that broke the twenty-homerun barriers. That same pair also drove in 100 RBI's each. This made the first combo to display power stats in homeruns and RBI's. Listed below are double play combinations with their power numbers.

Second Baseman and Shortstops with 100 RBI'S each in the Same Season

1934 Detroit *American League*	2B Charlie Gehringer	127
	SS Bill Rogell	100
1940 Boston *American League*	2B Bobby Doerr	105
	SS Joe Cronin	111
1948 Cleveland *American League*	2B Joe Gordon	124
	SS Lou Boudreau	106
1948 Boston *American League*	2B Bobby Doerr	111
	SS Vern Stephens	137
1949 Boston *American League*	2B Bobby Doerr	109
	SS Vern Stephens	159
1950 Boston *American League*	2B Bobby Doerr	120
	SS Vern Stephens	144

Second Basemen and Shortstops with Twenty Homeruns each in the Same Season

1940 Boston *American League*	2B Bobby Doerr	22
	SS Joe Cronin	24
1948 Boston *American League*	2B Bobby Doerr	27
	SS Vern Stephens	29
1950 Boston *American League*	2B Bobby Doerr	27
	SS Vern Stephens	30
1986 Detroit *American League*	2B Lou Whitaker	20
	SS Alan Trammell	21
1996 Baltimore *American League*	2B Roberto Alomar	20
	SS Cal Ripken	26

1994	Seattle *American League*	2B Dave Bell	20
		SS Alex Rodriguez	42
1999	San Francisco *National League*	2B Jeff Kent	22
		SS Rich Aurilia	22
2000	San Francisco *National League*	2B Jeff Kent	32
		SS Rich Aurilia	20
2001	San Francisco *National League*	2B Jeff Kent	22
		SS Rich Aurilia	37

Second Basemen and Shortstops with 20 Plus and 100 Plus RBI's in the Same Year

1940 Boston *American League*

Doerr	22 HR 105 RBI	151 Games	2B
Cronin	24 HR 111 RBI	146 Games	2B
		* Played two at 3B	

1948 Boston *American League*

| Doerr | 27 HR 111 RBI | 138 Games | 2B |
| Stephens | 29 HR 137 RBI | 155 Games | SS |

1950 Boston *American League*

| Doerr | 27 HR 120 RBI | 149 Games | 2B |
| Stephens | 30 HR 144 RBI | 146 Games | SS |

The Only Team with a Double Play Combination where both have More than 2000 Lifetime Hits.

In 1977, the Detroit Tigers were blessed with a rookie double play combination that would last nineteen years. Little did they know that both would be offensively and defensively proficient. Second baseman Lou Whitaker would retire in 1995, while shortstop Alan Trammell would call it quits the following year. Both retired with over 2000 hits making them the only double play combo in baseball history to claim that distinction.

		Hits
L. Whitaker	1977-1995	2369
A. Trammell	1977-1996	2365

Power Outfielders

Twice in the history of baseball were there teams in which all three outfielders had thirty or more homeruns in a season.

In the RBI category, only three teams had all three outfielders with one hundred or more RBI'S. In 2003, the Atlanta Braves became the only National League team to achieve the mark.

Thirty Home Run Outfielders

1941 New York Am. League		1963 Minnesota Am. League	
Charlie Keller	33	Harmon Killebrew	45
Tommy Henrich	31	Bob Allison	35
Joe DiMaggio	30	Jimmy Hall	32

Adjustment Made for Playing Other Positions and Pinch Hitting

100 RBI Outfields

1931 Detroit Am. League		1984 Boston Am. League	
Harry Heilman	139	Jim Rice	122
Bobby Veach	128	Tony Armas	108
Ty Cobb	100	Dwight Evans	104

Atlanta National League
Gary Sheffield
Andruw Jones
Chipper Jones
*Adjustments made for other positions, pinch hitting and designated hitting.

A note on the 1929 Chicago Cubs: it appears that their outfielders Hank Wilson, Riggs Stephenson and Kiki Cuyler, achieved the distinction of having three outfielders with 100 RBI'S each. Careful research found that Cuyler had three of his 102 RBI's as a pinch hitter. This left him with ninety-nine as an outfielder thus depriving the Cub's from becoming the first National League Team with three one hundred RBI outfielders

Triple Crown Winners in Batting and Pitching /Same Team in the Same Year

Only once in the modern times of baseball history has a team claimed the Triple Crown Batter (average, homeruns, RBI'S) and the Triple Crown pitcher (wins, strike- outs, ERA). This was accomplished by the 1934 New York Yankees. Lou Gehrig took the batting Triple Crown while "Lefty" Gomez copped the pitching Triple Crown. Ironically, the Yankees did not win the pennant that year.

	BA	HR	RBI
Gehrig	.363	49	165

	Wins	S.O.	ERA
Gomez	26	158	2.33

Teams with 400 Lifetime Homerun Hitters-Lefty and Right

Only two teams can claim this status. The Braves and Giants are the proud claimants.

Boston/Milwaukee/Atlanta			New York/San Francisco		
E. Matthews	(L)	493	W. Mays	(R)	646
H. Aaron	(R)	733	M. Ott	(L)	511

Teams with Lifetime 2500 Hit Men/Both Lefty and Righty

Only four teams can state they have a 2500 hit man from both sides of the plate. The Detroit Tigers is the only team that has a 3000 hit man from both sides.

American League

Detroit Tigers

| T. Cobb | (L) | 3900 |
| A. Kaline | (R) | 3007 |

National League

Chicago Cubs

A. Anson	(R)	3056
E. Banks	(R)	2583
B. Williams	(L)	2711

New York/San Francisco

| W. Mays | (R) | 3187 |
| M. Ott | (L) | 2896 |

Pittsburgh Pirates

H. Wagner	(R)	2967
R. Clemente	(R)	3000
P. Waner	(L)	2868

Teams with Thirty Home Run Hitters at Each Position (Excluding Pitchers)

Only two teams can claim this distinction: the Chicago Cubs and New York/San Francisco Giants. Three other teams need one position to be filled. They are Boston/Milwaukee/Atlanta, Cincinnati and the New York Yankees. The Braves and the Yankees need a shortstop, while the Reds need a second baseman. Note: Ernie Banks' name appears in positions because he hit thirty or more homers in different years while playing those positions. Fred McGriff hit thirty homers in 2002, but one was a double hitter, therefore he is ineligible for the list.

Thirty Home Runs Each Position

Chicago Cubs
1B Ernie Banks	1968	32
2B Roger Hornsby	1929	39
SS Ernie Banks	1958	47
3B Ron Santo	1965	33
C Gabby Hartnett	1930	37
OF Hack Wilson	1930	56
OF Billy Williams	1970	42
OF Sammy Sosa	1998	66

New York/San Francisco Giants
1B John Mize	1947	51
2B Jeff Kent	2002	37
SS Rich Aurila	2001	37
3B Matt Williams	1994	43
C Walker Cooper	1947	33
OF Barry Bonds	2001	73
OF Willie Mays	1965	52
OF Mel Ott	1929	42

Teams with 100 RBI Men at Every Position (Excluding Pitchers of Course)

Only five of the major league teams can fill a lineup of one hundred RBI men at every position. The selections made can, in most cases, have other players as replacements in most positions.

There are five other teams that are lacking at one position that need a one hundred-RBI man. Boston, Milwaukee/Atlanta, Cincinnati, Philadelphia and St. Louis all need a shortstop. Pittsburgh needs a catcher to complete their list.

100 RBI's Each Position

American League

Boston

Pos	Name	Year	RBI's
1B	Jimmy Foxx	1938	175
2B	Bobby Doerr	1950	120
SS	Joe Cronin	1939	107
3B	Frank Malzone	1957	103
C	Carlton Fisk	1977	102
OF	Ted Williams	1949	159
OF	Jackie Jensen	1958	122
OF	Jim Rice	1978	139

New York

Pos	Name	Year	RBI's
1B	Lou Gehrig	1931	184
2B	Tony Lazzeri	1930	121
SS	Derek Jeter	1999	102
3B	Craig Nettles	1977	107
C	Yogi Berra	1954	125
OF	Babe Ruth	1921	171
OF	Joe DiMaggio	1937	167
OF	Mickey Mantle	1950	130

National League

Brooklyn/Los Angeles Dodgers

Pos	Name	Year	RBI's
1B	Gil Hodges	1954	130
2B	Jackie Robinson	1949	124
SS	Glen Wright	1930	126
3B	Ron Cey	1977	110
C	Roy Campanella	1953	142
OF	Dixie Walker	1945	124
OF	Duke Snider	1955	136
OF	Carl Furillo	1950	106

Chicago Cubs

Pos	Name	Year	RBI's
1B	Ernie Banks	1969	106
2B	Rogers Hornsby	1929	149
SS	Ernie Banks	1959	143
3B	Ron Santo	1969	123
C	Gabby Hartnett	1930	122
OF	Hack Wilson	1930	191
OF	Sammy Sosa	2001	160
OF	Billy Williams	1970	129

New York/San Francisco Giants

Pos	Name	Year	RBI's
1B	John Mize	1947	138
2B	Rogers Hornsby	1927	125
SS	Travis Jackson	1934	101
3B	Fred Lindstrom	1928	107
C	Walker Cooper	1947	122
OF	Willie Mays	1962	141
OF	Mel Ott	1929	151
OF	Barry Bonds	2001	137

Teams with Hall of Famers at each Position.
(They must have played a full year at one position.)

Only four teams can boast that they can field an All-Star team with Hall Of Famers at each position. These are the Boston Red Sox and the New York Yankees in the American League and the New York/San Francisco Giants and Pittsburgh Pirates in the National League. Three teams need one player to complete their lineup of Hall of Famers. They are Milwaukee/St. Louis/Baltimore, the Chicago Cubs and the St. Louis Cardinals. Baltimore needs a second baseman, and Chicago and St. Louis both need a third baseman.

Some Cub fans might argue the case for Fred Lindstrom, but the year he played for the Cubs, most of his games were elsewhere.

Teams with Hall Of Famers at Each Position:

<u>New York Yankees</u>
1B	Lou Gehrig
2B	Tony Lazzeri/Joe Gordon
SS	Phil Rizzuto
3B	Joe Sewell/Frank Baker
C	Bill Dickey/Yogi Berra
OF	Babe Ruth/Reggie Jackson
OF	Joe DiMaggio/Earle Combs
OF	Mickey Mantle
P	Ford/Gomez/Gossage/ Hoyt/ Pennock/Ruffing

<u>Pittsburgh</u>
1B	Willie Stargell
2B	Bill Mazeroski
SS	Honus Wagner
3B	Pie Traynor
C	Al Lopez
OF	Paul Waner
OF	Lloyd Waner
OF	Roberto Clemente
P	Burleigh Grimes

<u>New York/San Francisco Giants</u>
1B	Bill Terry
2B	Frankie Frisch
SS	Travis Jackson
3B	Fred Lindstrom
C	Roger Bresnahan
OF	Mel Ott
OF	Willie Mays
OF	Ross Youngs
P	C.Mathewson/C. Hubbell

<u>Boston Red Sox</u>
1B	Jimmy Foxx
2B	Bobby Doerr
SS	Joe Cronin
3B	Jimmy Collins
C	Carlton Fisk
OF	Ted Williams
OF	Tris Speaker
OF	Harry Hooper
P	Cy Young

Teams with four Hall of Famers on their Pitching Staff

A team that has even two or three Hall of Fame pitchers on a staff must make a manager feel overly secure. Only two of the four teams listed below won the pennant, therefore to have immortals does not guarantee they're headed for the World Series.

National League

St. Louis 1934
D. Dean	30-7	
J. Haines	4-4	
B. Grimes	2-1	(Traded during season)
D. Vance	1-1	

American League

New York 1930
R. Ruffing	15-5
H. Pennock	11-7
W. Hoyt	2-2
L. Gomez	2-5

Cleveland 1949
B. Lemon	22-10
B. Feller	15-14
E. Wynn	11-7
S. Paige	4-7

Cleveland 1954
B. Lemon	23- 7
E. Wynn	23-11
B. Feller	13 -3
H. Newhouser	7 -2

Teams with Two Thirty Game Winners Since 1900

Before 1900, five teams in the National League had two thirty game winners on their staff. This was also accomplished five times in the American Association. The Players League in its one year existence had one team with two thirty game winners.

After 1900, the New York Giants with Christy Mathewson and Joe McGinnity both topped the thirty-victory mark. They did it in consecutive years--matching the Boston Beaneaters of 1891 and 1892. The St. Louis Browns of 1885 and 1886 had two pitchers who also won 30 plus games in consecutive years.

Mathewson and McGinnity are the two to do it in modern times, and at the pitching distance of 60' 6".

New York 1903		New York 1904	
J. McGinnity	31-20	J. McGinnity	35-8
C. Mathewson	31-13	C. Mathewson	33-12

Multiple Twenty Game Winners on the Same Pitching Staff

Where the shutouts and complete games are statistics that are becoming extinct for the individual pitcher so is the number of multiple twenty-game winners on a team's staff. Only since the 1990's can six teams boast of having two twenty game winners the same year. Five of these are in the National League (Atlanta 1993, of 1993, Houston 1998, Arizona 2001, Arizona 2002.) Boston had a pair of twenty gamers in 2002.

The history of the game shows that on twenty-two occasions, teams had three or more aces that hit the twenty marks. Twice in the game's history, there were four that made the charmed circle, but that many stalwarts did not ensure a team a pennant. Only eleven of the twenty-two staffs propelled their team to a pennant.

Please note that baseball stats during the early years of the game often conflict in resource materials. The Philadelphia Phillies of 1901 and Philadelphia A's of 1905 are examples. The Phillies' B. Duggleby is listed as a twenty game winner in half of the resource material; therefore he is on the list. A. Coakley is listed as a twenty game winner in one book while all others list him with less than twenty wins. The A's of 1905 are not listed.

Teams with Three or More Twenty Game Winners

American League

Boston 1903		Boston 1904	
C. Young	28-9	C. Young	26-16
T. Hughes	20-7	B. Dinneen	23-14
B. Dinneen	21-11	J. Tannenhill	21-11

Cleveland 1906		Chicago 1907	
B. Rhoads	22-10	D. White	27-13
A. Joss	21-9	E. Walsh	24-18
O. Hess	20-17	F. Smith	22-11

Detroit 1907		Chicago 1920	
B. Donovan	25-4	J. Faber	23-13
E. Killian	25-13	C. Williams	22-14
G. Mullin	20-20	D. Kerr	21-9
		E. Cicotte	21-10

Cleveland 1920		Philadelphia 1931	
J. Bagby	31-12	R. Grove	31-4
S. Coveleski	24-14	G. Earnshaw	21-7
R. Caldwell	20-10	G. Walberg	20-12

Cleveland 1951		Cleveland 1952	
R. Feller	22-8	E. Wynn	23-12
E. Wynn	20-13	R. Lemon	22-11
M. Garcia	20-13	M. Garcia	22-11

Cleveland 1956		Baltimore 1970	
E. Wynn	20-9	M. Cuellar	24-8
H. Score	20-9	D. McNally	24-9
R. Lemon	20-14	J. Palmer	20-10

Baltimore 1971			Oakland 1973	
D. McNally	21-5		J. Hunter	21-5
P. Dobson	20-8		K. Holtzman	21-13
M. Cuellar	20-9		V. Blue	20-9
J. Palmer	20-9			

National League

Philadelphia 1901			Chicago 1903	
A. Orth	20-12		J. Taylor	21-14
B. Duggleby	20-12	*	J. Weimer	20-8
R. Donahue	20-13		B. Wicker	20-9

New York 1904			New York 1905	
J. McGinnity	35-8		A. Mathewson	32-8
C. Mathewson	33-12		J. McGinnity	22-16
D. Taylor	21-15		R. Ames	22-8

New York 1913			New York 1920	
C. Mathewson	25-11		F. Toney	21-11
R. Marquard	23-10		A. Nehf	21-12
J. Tesreau	22-13		J. Barnes	20-15

Cincinnati 1923	
C. Luque	27-8
P. Donohue	21-15
D. Rixey	20-15

Federal League

St. Louis 1915	
D. Davenport	22-18
E. Plank	21-11
D. Crandall	21-15

Teams with Two or More 200 Strikeout Pitchers

We tend to label power pitchers as those who break the two hundred-strikeout barriers. Starting in the 1960's, the strikeout aces emerged frequently and quite often teams would have more than one who would top the two hundred mark. Prior to the 1960's, only three times in the game's history did teams have two 200-strikeout artists. Only twice in the history of the game did a team produce more than two. Note that only once has a team had two three hundred-strikeout men.

American League

1904 Philadelphia			1904 New York		
R. Waddell	349		J. Chesbro		239
E. Plank	201		A. Orth		202

1905 Philadelphia			1967 Minnesota		
R. Waddell	287		D. Chance		220
E. Plank	210		J. Kaat	211	
			D. Boswell		204

1967 Cleveland			Cleveland		
S. McDowell	236		S. McDowell		283
L. Tiant	219		L. Tiant		264

1971 Detroit			1971 Chicago		
M. Lolich	308		W. Wood		210
J. Coleman	236		T. Bradley		206

1972 Detroit			1973 Detroit		
M. Lolich	250		M. Lolich		214
J. Coleman	222		J. Coleman		202

1973 California			1976 California		
N. Ryan	383		N. Ryan		327
B. Singer	241		F. Tanana		261

1977 California			1986 California		
N. Ryan	341		M. Witt		208
F. Tanana	205		K. McCaskill		202

1990 Texas		2001 New York	
N. Ryan	232	M. Mussina	214
B. Witt	221	R. Clemens	213

2004 Boston		2008 Toronto	
P .Martinez	227	A. Burnett	231
C. Schilling	203	R. Halladay	206

2011 Tampa Bay		2012 Detroit	
J. Shields	225	J. Verlander	239
D. Price	218	M. Scherzer	231

2013 Detroit	
M. Scherzer	240
J. Verlander	217
A. Sanchez	202

National League

1961 Los Angeles		1962 Los Angeles	
S. Koufax	269	D. Drysdale	232
S. Williams	205	S. Koufax	216

1963 Los Angeles		1964 Los Angeles	
S. Koufax	306	D. Drysdale	237
D. Drysdale	251	S. Koufax	223

1965 Los Angeles		1965 Philadelphia	
S. Koufax	382	J. Bunning	268
D. Drysdale	210	C. Short	237

1966 Los Angeles		1966 San Francisco	
S. Koufax	317	J. Marichal	222
D. Sutton	209	G. Perry	201

1968 San Francisco		1969 San Francisco	
J. Marichal	218	G. Perry	233
G. Perry	206	J. Marichal	205

1969 St. Louis		1969 Houston	
B. Gibson	269	D. Wilson	235
S. Carlton	210	L. Dierker	232
		T. Griffin 200	

1969 Los Angeles		1973 New York	
B. Singer	247	T. Seaver	251
D. Sutton	217	J. Matlock	205

1976 New York		1986 New York	
T. Seaver	235	D. Gooden	200
J. Koosman	200	S. Fernandez	200

1990 New York		1996 Houston	
D. Cone	233	D. Kile	219
D. Gooden	223	S. Reynolds	204

1996 Montreal		2000 Los Angeles	
P. Martinez	222	C. Park	217
J. Fassero	222	K. Brown	216

2001 Arizona		2002 Arizona	
R. Johnson	372	R. Johnson	334
C. Schilling	293	C. Schilling	316

2002 Chicago		2003 Chicago	
K. Wood	217	K. Wood	266
M. Clement	215	M. Prior	245

2004 Houston		2010 Philadelphia	
R. Clemens	218	R. Halladay	219
R. Oswalt	206	C. Hamels	211

2010 San Francisco		2011 Milwaukee	
T. Lincecum	231	Y. Gallardo	207
J. Sanchez	205	Z. Greinke	201

2011 Philadelphia		2012 Philadelphia	
C. Lee	238	C. Hamels	216
R. Halladay	220	C. Lee	207

2013 Philadelphia		*Federal League*	
C. Lee	222	1914 Indianapolis	
C. Hamels	202	C. Falkenberg	236
		E. Moseley	205

The Only Teams with 2000 Lifetime Strike Out Pitchers As Right Handed and Left Handed

Only three teams can claim the distinction of having a right-hander and left-hander with 2000 lifetime strikeouts.

American League

Cleveland
B. Feller   (R) 2581
S. McDowell   (L) 2159

National League

Boston/Milwaukee/Atlanta   Brooklyn/Los Angeles
P. Niekro   (R) 3048   D. Drysdale   (R) 2486
W. Spahn   (L) 2493   S. Koufax   (L) 2396

Pitching Futility

In 2003, Mike Maroth of the Detroit Tigers became the first twenty game loser since Brian Kingman went 8-20 in 1980 for the Oakland A's. This is not so shocking when you come to realize that since 1900, teams with two or more twenty game losers occurred twenty-four times, with the National League leading the way with twelve teams. To add insult to injury, the Boston Beaneaters had four twenty-game losses twice and that was done in consecutive years. Four other teams had three twenty-game losses and the Boston Beaneaters were one of them.

National League

1904 Brooklyn   1905 Boston
Oscar Jones   17-25   Vic Willis   11-29
Jack Cronin   12-23   Kaiser Wilhelm   4-23
                                  Irv Young   20-21

1905 Brooklyn   1905 Boston
Harry McIntire 8-25   Vic Willis   18-25
Mal Eason   5-21   Kaiser Wilhelm   15-21
                                  Togie Pittinger   14-21
                                  Chick Fraser   14-21

1906 Boston			1908 Brooklyn	
Irv. Young	16-25		Kaiser Wilhelm	18-22
Gus Dorner	8-25		Harry McIntire	11-20
Vive Lindaman	12-23		Jim Pastorius	4-20
Jeff Pfeffer	13-22			

1909 Boston			1913 St. Louis	
Cecil Ferguson	5-23		Dan Griner	10-22
Al Mattern	16-20		Bob Harmon	8-21

1920 Boston			1936 Philadelphia	
Dana Fillingim	12-21		Bucky Walters	11-21
Jack Scott	10-21		Joe Bowman	9-20

1962 New York			1965 New York	
Roger Craig	10-24		Jack Fisher	8-24
Al Jackson	8-20		Al Jackson	8-20

American League

1903 Washington			1904 Washington	
Casey Patten	10-23		Jack Townsend	5-27
Al Orth	0-21		Beany Jacobson	5-23
			Casey Patten	15-21

1904 Detroit			1905 St. Louis	
George Mullin	16-24		Fred Glade	7-24
Ed Killian	15-20		Joe Harris	2-21
			Willie Sudhoff	10-20

1906 Boston			1908 New York	
Cy Young	13-21		Joe Lake	9-22
Jack Chesbro	14-20		Harry Howell	14-21

1909 Washington			1916 Philadelphia	
Bob Groom	7-26		Joe Bush	15-24
Walter Johnson	13-25		Elmer Myers	14-23

1920 Philadelphia			1930 Boston	
Scott Perry	11-25		Milt Gaston	13-20
Rollie Naylor	10-23		Jack Russell	9-20

1973 Chicago		
Stan Bahnsen	18-21	
Wilbur Wood	24-20	

1914 St. Louis
Bob Groom   13-20
Hank Keupper   8-20

Twenty Game Losers for Pennant Winners

It boggles the imagination when thinking that a twenty game loser can contribute to a team's success as a pennant winner. It has happened three times in the game's history. It occurred twice during the 1880's when teams had two or three man rotations. Only one in modern baseball was accomplished.

1883 Jim Whitney Boston NL 37-21

1888 Charles King St Louis AL 45-21

1907 George Mullin Detroit AL 20-20

Teams with Three or more Shutout Leaders in the Same Year

In 1924, the Pittsburgh Pirates became the first major league team to have three pitchers on the same staff lead the league in shutouts. The year 1929 saw the St. Louis Browns duplicate the feat. To this day, they are the only American league team to claim that distinction. To top those achievements the Chicago Cubs of 1936, had the four starters of their rotation leaf the league in shutouts. Listed below are the teams with three or more shutout leaders.

National League

Chicago 1936		Pittsburgh 1924		New York 1950	
L. French	4	W. Cooper	4	S. Maglie	5
B. Lee	4	R. Kremer	4	L. Jansen	5
L. Warneke	4	E. Yde	4	J. Hearn	5
T. Carleton	4				

American League

Milwaukee 1959		St. Louis 1929	
W. Spahn	4	S. Gray	4
L. Burdette	4	A. Crowder	4
B. Buhl	4	G. Blaeholder	4

Most Teams Having a Shutout Leader in the Same Year

The 1921 National League produced an oddity in which seven of the eight teams had a pitcher who led the league in shutouts.

D. Fillingim	Boston	3
J. Oeschger	Boston	3
C. Mitchell	Brooklyn	3
G. Alexander	Chicago	3
D. Luque	Cincinnati	3
P. Douglas	New York	3
J. Morrison	Pittsburgh	3
J. Haines	St. Louis	3

L. Meadows of the Philadelphia Phillies had two.

Pennant and Division Winners Who Finished Twenty or More Games Ahead of Second Place Finishers

In 1902, the Pittsburgh Pirates leap-frogged to the pennant over the second place Brooklyn Superbras by the twenty-seventh and a half game. The Chicago Cubs of 1906 also ran away from the pack with a spread of twenty games over the New York Giants. These are the only teams to win a pennant by that margin.

Since division play began in 1969, only seven times did a first place have an expanse of twenty or more games. In 1995, the Cleveland Indians set the record for capturing first place by thirty games.

American League	GA		National League	GA
1983 Chicago	20		*1902 Pittsburgh	27 1/2

29

*1995	Cleveland	30	*1906	Chicago	20
*1998	New York	22	*1975	Cincinnati	20
1999	Cleveland	21 1/2	*1986	New York	21 1/2
			*1995	Atlanta	21

*Won Pennant

Only Teams with 200 Game Winners
as Right Handed and Left Handed

To win two hundred is a splendid achievement even though it has been done close to one hundred times. Only five teams can claim the fact that they have both a right-hander and a left-hander to accomplish the two hundred-win milestone. Listed below are those teams, with Detroit showing a duet from both-sides.

American League

Detroit			New York		
G. Mullin	(R)	209	R. Ruffing	(R)	231
G. Dauss	(R)	222	W. Ford	(L)	236
M. Lolich	(L)	207	A. Pettitte*	(L)	218
H. Newhouser	(L)	200			

*Active Player

National League

Boston/Milwaukee/Atlanta			New York/ San Francisco		
P. Niekro	(R)	268	C. Mathewson	(R)	372
J. Smoltz	(R)	210	J. Marichal	(R)	238
W. Spahn	(L)	356	C. Hubbell	(L)	253
T. Glavine	(L)	244			

Philadelphia		
R. Roberts	(R)	234
S. Carlton	(L)	241

From 1892 through 2003, a team winning one hundred or more games occurred ninety-one times. It happened only three times in the nineteenth century. The Boston Beaneaters did this in 1892 and 1898. In 1899, the

Brooklyn Superbras topped the one hundred-win mark. Scanning the records, we see that in 1892 the season was played in two halves. Boston won the first half with a fifty-two to twenty-two record. The second half winner was Cleveland with fifty-three to twenty-three marks. Boston finished second with a fifty to twenty-six ledger. The two winners would meet for the season championship. This was to continue post season play because the World Series between the National League and American Association was now ended. This was due to the Association demise because of financial failure.

Boston's total record for the year was one hundred and two to forty-eight. Their forty-eighth win in the second half was their hundredth of the year. To prepare for the championship, manager Frank Selee used his three starters for short stints. Boston's three hurlers were, in order, Staley (three innings), Nichols (two innings), and Stivetts who pitched the last four, shutting out Baltimore. This gave Stivetts the win, thus becoming the first pitcher in history to win a team's hundredth game. Please note that Gabriel Schechter of baseball's hall of fame supplied this information.

In 1898, Boston again won over a hundred games: this time Nichols gained the victory.

In 1899, Brooklyn won one hundred-one games. There is an oddity since gaining the hundredth win was a forfeited game against Baltimore. The Orioles took a one to zero lead early in the game on a single by Jimmy Sheckard. Sheckard was in a close race for the stolen base lead. He took off for a second and was thrown out according to umpire Hunt. Sheckard erupted and pushed the arbitrator. When ordered to leave the game, Sheckard defied the order and remained on the field. The umpire had no other recourse but to call the game as a forfeit for Brooklyn, therefore giving them their hundredth win.

Bedlam then continued when the fan objected to having to pay for a forfeit. To quiet the ruckus that was bent on becoming a major riot, the powers that be remembered that the two teams had a rainout during the season. They used that game to appease the fans. Brooklyn won that eight to three, which gave them one hundred and one victories on games actually played.

Since modern baseball began (circa 1900) the American League has seen teams win one hundred games forty times, while the National witnessed forty-two of their members crack the one hundred mark. The Pittsburgh Pirates were the first to accomplish the defeat in 1902. The Philadelphia A's became the first American League contingent in 1910 to rise to that level.

There are a few unique achievements in winning a team's hundredth victory. George Pipgras, pitching for the New York Yankees, became the first and only American leaguer to win his teams' hundredth victory twice -- in 1928 and 1932.

Pipgras' feat was duplicated in the National League three times the following year:

Mort Cooper St. Louis	1942, 1944
Jim Lonborg Philadelphia	1976, 1977
Tom Glavine Atlanta	1998, 1999

It should be noted that Lonborg and Glavine are the only pitchers who did it in consecutive years. Another strange occurrence happened in 1909 when Nick Maddox with Pittsburgh captured his team's one hundredth win. The irony for Maddox was he became the loser when the Chicago Cubs won their one hundredth. This gave Maddox the distinction of being the only pitcher to suffer this scenario in the same season.

In 1954, Moe Burtschy of the Philadelphia A's was the loser in two teams' hundredth wins. Cleveland and New York cracked the century mark and poor Moe aided both of them in the accomplishment. Just for the record, the Philly A's, in their last year in the city of brotherly love, lost one hundred and three games. Moe was the only pitcher with a winning record for that pitiful bunch.

Not to let Moe wallow alone in an undignified accomplishment, Len Barker, with Cleveland in 1980, duplicated Moe's mark. Barker lost both one hundred game victories that New York and Baltimore achieved. However, Barker's losses were more painful than Moe's. If he won one of those contests, he would have gained his twenty victories for the only time in his career.

Listed below are all the hundredth wins:

American League

Team	Year	Opponent	Score	WP	LP	Total Wins
Philadelphia	1910	Boston	3-0	Russell	Collins	102
Philadelphia	1911	New York	1-0	Morgan	Quinn	101
Boston	1912	New York	6-0	Wood	Shulz	105
Boston	1915	New York	2-0	Hughes	Palmero	101
Detroit	1915	Cleveland	6-5	James	Jones	100
Chicago	1917	New York	3-1	Cicotte	Thormahlen	
New York	1927	Chicago	7-2	Moore	Blankenship	110
New York	1928	Detroit	11-6	Pipgras	Gibson	101
Philadelphia	1929	Detroit	10-7	Yerkes	Prudhomme	104
Philadelphia	1930	St Louis	10-4	Shores	Gray	102
Philadelphia	1931	Cleveland	7-5	Eranshaw	Terrell	107
New York	1932	Cleveland	9-3	Pipgras	Brown	107
Detroit	1934	St Louis	10-6	Crowder	Newsom	101
New York	1936	Philadelphia	12-5	Broaca	Turbeville	102
New York	1937	Philadelphia	15-4	Wicker	Caster	102
New York	1939	Chicago	6-2	Hildebrand	Smith	106
New York	1941	Washington	4-1	Chandler	Chase	101
New York	1942	Detroit	7-4	Donald	Trout	103
Boston	1946	Washington	7-5	Zuber	Haefner	104
Cleveland	1954	Philadelphia	5-4	Newhouser	Burtschy	111
New York	1954	Philadelphia	4-2	Sain	Burtschy	103
New York	1961	Chicago	4-3	Terry	Pierce	109
Detroit	1961	Minnesota	6-4	Koplitz	Kaat	101
New York	1963	Minnesota	2-1	Ford	Stange	104
Minnesota	1965	Baltimore	3-2	Grant	Barber	102
Detroit	1968	Washington	6-3	Lolich	Huphreys	103
Baltimore	1969	Cleveland	2-1	Hardin	Williams	109
Baltimore	1970	Detroit	10-2	Phoebus	Reed	108
Baltimore	1971	Boston	5-4	Richert	Peters	101
Oakland	1971	KC	2-1	Hunter	Hedlund	101
New York	1977	Detroit	8-7	Thomas	Foucault	100
KC	1977	California	6-3	Gura	Simpson	102

New York	1978	Boston	5-4	Guidry	Torrez	100
Baltimore	1979	Cleveland	7-3	Flanagan	Spillner	102
New York	1980	Cleveland	18-7	Perry	Barker	103
Baltimore	1980	Cleveland	7-1	McGregor	Barker	100
Detroit	1984	New York	4-1	Morris	Fontenot	104
Oakland	1988	Milwaukee	5-2	Stewart	Wegman	104
Oakland	1990	Texas	4-1	Moore	Hough	103
Cleveland	1995	Chicago	19-7	Nagy	Gordon	100
New York	1998	Chicago	11-6	Lloyd	Bradford	114
Seattle	2001	Tampa Bay	12-6	Halama	Phelps	116
Oakland	2001	Anaheim	6-2	Hudson	Ortiz	102
New York	2002	Tampa Bay	4-3	Weaver	Sturtze	103
Oakland	2002	Seattle	5-3	Koch	Hasegawa	103
New York	2003	Baltimore	6-2	Clemens	Johnson	101
New York	2004	Toronto	3-2	Proctor	Towers	101
Los Angeles	208	Texas	7-0	Saunders	Millwood	100
New York	2004	Tampa Bay	10-2	Burnett	Davis	103

National League

Team	Year	Opponent	Score	WP	LP	Total Wins
Pittsburgh	1902	St Louis	4-1	Leever	Morrissey	103
New York	1904	Cincinnati	7-5	McGinnity	Kellum	106
New York	1905	St Louis	6-5	Mathewson	Theilman	105
Chicago	1906	Pittsburgh	7-2	Pfiester	Leever	116
Chicago	1907	Boston	8-7	Lundgren	Dessau	107
Pittsburgh	1909	Brooklyn	12-3	Maddox	Knetzer	110
Chicago	1909	Pittsburgh	3-1	Reulbach	Maddox	104
Chicago	1910	Pittsburgh	5-3	McIntire	Steele	104
New York	1912	Boston	7-6	Kirby	Dickson	103
New York	1913	Philadelphia	12-7	Crandall	Marshall	101
St Louis	1931	Cincinnati	6-2	Derringer	Lucas	101
Chicago	1935	St Louis	5-3	Henshaw	Ryba	100
Cincinnati	1940	Pittsburgh	11-3	Walters	Rambert	100
Brooklyn	1941	Philadelphia	5-1	Chipman	Melton	100
St Louis	1942	Chicago	1-0	Cooper	Warneke	106
Brooklyn	1942	Philadelphia	6-0	French	Melton	104
St Louis	1943	Boston	7-1	Lanier	Javaery	105

34

St Louis	1944	Philadelphia	4-3	Cooper	Raffensberger	105
Brooklyn	1953	St Louis	4-3	Erksine	Haddix	105
San Francisco	1962	Houston	11-5	Sanford	Johnson	103
Los Angeles	1962	St Louis	4-1	Podres	Washurn	102
St Louis	1967	Atlanta	3-1	Hughes	Britton	101
New York	1969	Chicago	6-5	Taylor	Selma	100
Cincinnati	1970	Los Angeles	6-3	Gullet	Sutton	102
Los Angeles	1974	San Diego	5-2	Messersmith	Grief	102
Cincinnati	1975	Atlanta	4-3	Borbon	Torrealba	108
Philadelphia	1976	New York	7-4	Lonborg	Matlock	101
Cincinnati	1976	San Diego	5-4	Billingham	Sawyer	102
Philadelphia	1977	Montreal	9-4	Lonborg	Bahnsen	101
St Louis	1985	Chicago	4-2	Forsch	Eckersley	101
New York	1986	Chicago	6-5	McDowell	Lynch	108
New York	1988	St Louis	7-5	Darling	McWilliams	100
San Francisco	1993	Colorado	6-4	Hickerson	Nied	103
Atlanta	1993	Philadelphia	7-2	Avery	Schilling	104
Atlanta	1997	Philadelphia	3-2	Cather	Spradlin	101
Houston	1998	St Louis	7-1	Johnson	Oliver	102
Atlanta	1998	Arizona	5-0	Glavine	Anderson	106
Arizona	1999	San Diego	10-3	Anderson	Murray	100
Atlanta	1999	New York	9-3	Glavine	Hershiser	103
Atlanta	2002	New York	7-4	Millwood	Astacio	101
San Francisco	2003	Los Angeles	12-3	Correia	Alavarez	100
Atlanta	2003	Philadelphia	6-0	Ramirez	Padilla	100
St Louis	2004	Milwaukee	4-2	Eldred	Wise	105
St Louis	2005	Cincinnati	7-5	Thompson	Claussen	100

In baseball, there have been seven streaks of twenty or more games without a loss. These include ties. The first steak of twenty or more games of a team being undefeated occurred in 1880, when the Chicago White Stockings went twenty-two games before tasting defeat. Included in that total is one tie. During those years, teams usually had no more than a two-man rotation. Chicago's two aces, Larry Corcoran (thirteen wins) and Fred Goldsmith (eight wins), reaped the benefit in all the decisions.

Twice in 1884, there were two streaks of exactly twenty games. One happened in the Union Association in its only year of existence. The St. Louis Maroons started the season winning their first twenty games. The U.A. was not a league of parity because the Maroons were basically a stacked team.

In the National, the Providence Grays steam-rolled their way to the 1884 pennant on the right arm of Charles "Old Hoss" Radbourn. He produced sixty wins with eighteen of them coming in Providences' twenty game winning streaks.

The next time a twenty game skein occurred was in the American League. The "Hit Less Wonders" Chicago White Sox in 1906 went twenty games without a loss. The one blemish was a zero to zero tie, with their nearest competitor for the pennant, the New York Highlanders.

The 1916 New York Giants had gone twenty-seven games without a loss. They would set the record for the longest winning streak of twenty games. Included in the statistic is a one to one tie with Pittsburgh that was ended by rain. An oddity of this streak was that all games were played at home.

The Giants would have a streak of seventeen victories earlier in the year all coming on the road. The most peculiar thing of all was that the Giants finished the year in fourth place.

The next streak of twenty plus would come in 1935, when the Chicago Cubs would catapult themselves through the month of September with twenty-one in a row. This all but insured the pennant to the Cubs.
In 2002, the Oakland A's laid claim to the American League record by winning twenty games in a row. The last three games were seesaw affairs, as the A's closer, Billy Koch, gained all three victories.

1880 Chicago Twenty-One Game

A 6/2	Chicago	5	Boston	4	Corcoran	Foley
A 6/5	Chicago	6	Pro	3	Goldsmith	Ward
A 6/6	Chicago	1	Pro	1		
A 6/7	Chicago	7	Pro	1	Corcoran	Ward
A 6/8	Chicago	6	Pro	4	Goldsmith	Ward
A 6/10	Chicago	8	Troy	5	Corcoran	Welch

A 6/11 Chicago	10	Troy	4	Goldsmith	Welch
A 6/14 Chicago	16	Troy	2	Corcoran	
A6/16 Chicago	10	Worc.	6	Goldsmith	Richmond
A 6/17 Chicago	11	Worc	8	Corcoran	Richmond
A 6/19 Chicago	8	Worc	7	Corcoran	Richmond
H 6/22 Chicago	5	Troy	2	Corcoran	Welch
H 6/23 Chicago	10	Troy	4	Goldsmith	Welch
H 6/24 Chicago	9	Troy	3	Corcoran	Welch
H 6/26 Chicago	4	Worc	0	Corcoran	Richmond
H 6/28 Chicago	4	Worc	1	Corcoran	Richmond
H 6/29 Chicago	9	Worc	5	Corcoran	Richmond
H 7/2 Chicago	10	Boston	3	Goldsmith	Foley
H 7/3 Chicago	6	Boston	1	Corcoran	Bond
H 7/5 Chicago	3	Prov	2	Goldsmith	Bradley
H 7/6 Chicago	7	Prov	1	Corcoran	Ward
H 7/8 Chicago	5	Prov	4	Corcoran	Ward

On 7/10, the streak ended at Cleveland with Chicago losing two to zero.
The winner was McCormick and the loser Goldsmith. St. Louis Union
Association 1884, Twenty Game Win Streak

H 4/20	Chicago	7-2	Hodnett	Daily
H 4/24	Atloona	11-2	Werden	Brown
H 4/26	Atloona	9-3	Taylor	Leary
H 4/27	Atloona	7-1	Hodett	Murphy
H 4/28	Atloona	8-1	Taylor	Brown
A 4/30	Atloona	15-2	Hodnett	Murphy
A 5/2	Atloona	16/3	Taylor	Leary
A 5/3	Atloona	14-5	Hodnett	Conners
A 5/5	Atloona	12-2	Taylor	Brown
H 5/8	Washington	22-2	Hodnett	Lockwood
H 5/9	Washington	12-4	Taylor	Wise
H 5/10	Washington	8-4	Hodnett	Voss
H 5/11	Washington	11-6	Taylor	Lockwood
H 5/14	Baltimore	7-5	Hodnett	W. Sweeney
H 5/15	Baltimore	20-6	Taylor	W. Sweeney
H 5/17	Baltimore	16-8	Werden	W. Sweeney
H 5/18	Baltimore	6-3	Taylor	W. Sweeney
H 5/21	Boston	12-3	Hodnett	Bond
H 5/22	Boston	16-4	Taylor	Burke

H 5/23	Boston	4-1	Taylor	Burke

The streak came to an end 5/24/84 at St. Louis when Boston won eight to one. Bonds defeated Hodnett.

Providence Twenty Game Win Streak 1884

A 8/7	New York	4-2	Radbourn	Dorgan (ML Debut)
A 8/8	Philadelphia	6-0	Conley	McElroy
A 8/9	Boston	1-0	Radbourn	Buffington 11inns
H 8/11	Boston	3-1	Radbourn	Whitney
A 8/12	Boston	4-0	Radbourn	Buffington
H 8/14	Boston	1-0	Radbourn	Buffington
H 8/15	Cleveland	3-2	Radbourn	Harkins
H 8/19	Detroit	4-2	Radbourn	Weidman
H 8/20	Detroit	5-2	Conley	Getzein
H 8/21	Chicago	5-3	Radbourn	Corcoran
H 8/23	Chicago	7-3	Radbourn	Corcoran
H 8/27	Chicago	5-3	Radbourn	Clarkson
H 8/28	Chicago	8-4	Radbourn	Corcoran
H 8/29	Detroit	7-1	Radbourn	Meinke
H 8/30	Detroit	6-5	Radbourn	Weidman
				Prov Scored in Bottom 11th
H 9/2	Buffalo	4-0	Radbourn	Galvin
H 9/3	Buffalo	10-1	Radbourn	Serad
H 9/4	Cleveland	3-1	Radbourn	Moffett
H 9/5	Cleveland	5-4	Radbourn	Henry
H 9/6	Cleveland	3-0	Radbourn	Moffett

The streak stopped 9/9/84 when Buffalo won two to zero. Galvin beat Radbourn.

H 8/2/06	Chicago	3	Boston	0	White	Young
H 8/3/06	Chicago	4	Boston	0	Walsh	Harris
H 8/4/06	Chicago	1	Boston	0	Patterson	Dineen
H 8/5/06	Chicago	10	Philadelphia	2	White	Bendel
H 8/6/06	Chicago	7	Philadelphia	2	Owen	Coombs
H 8/7/06	Chicago	4	Philadelphia	0	Walsh	Wadell
H 8/8/06	Chicago	1	Philadelphia	0	Patterson	Plank
H 8/9/06	Chicago	3	Philadelphia	2	White	Dygert
H 8/10/06	Chicago	2	New York	1	Walsh	Chesbro
H 8/11/06	Chicago	8	New York	1	Owen	Hogg
H 8/12/06	Chicago	3	New York	0	Walsh	Orth

H 8/13/06	Chicago	0	New York 0	White	Chesbro (tie)	
A 8/15/06	Chicago	5	Boston 0 Walsh	J. Tannehill		
A 8/16/06	Chicago	9	Boston 4 Altrock	Harris		
A 8/17/06	Chicago	4	Boston 3 Owen Started –White/Young			
A 8/18/06	Chicago	10	New York0 Walsh	Chesbro		
A 8/20/06	Chicago	4	New York 1 White	Orth		
A 8/22/06	Chicago	6	New York 1 White	Orth		
A 8/22/06	Chicago	11	New York 6 Owen	Hogg		

Double Header

A 8/23/06	Chicago	4	Washington 1 Patterson	Falkenberg	

The streak ended when Washington won a double-header 8/25/06. Washington 5, Chicago 3, WP Patten LP /White in relief.

1916 NY Giants Twenty-six Game Win Streak

H 9/7	New York	4	Brooklyn	1	Schupp	Rucker
H 9/8	New York	9	Philadelphia	3	Tesreau	Alexander
H 9/9	New York	3	Philadelphia	1	Perritt	Demaree
H 9/9	New York	3	Philadelphia	10	Perritt	Bender
H 9/11	New York	9	Philadelphia		Tesreau	Rixey
H 9/12	New York	3	Cincinnati	2	Benton	Mitchell
H 9/13	New York	3	Cincinnati	4	Smith	Schneider
H 9/14	New York	3	Cincinnati	1	Tesreau	Moseley
H 9/16	New York	8	Pittsburgh	2	Benton	Mamaux
H 9/16	New York	4	Pittsburgh	3	Tesreau	Cooper
H 9/18	New York	2	Pittsburgh	0	Schupp	Miller
H 9/18	New York	1	Pittsburgh	1	Perritt	Grimes

(tie) 8 inning rain

H 9/19	New York	9	Pittsburgh	2	Benton	Jacobs
H 9/19	New York	5	Pittsburgh	1	Tesreau	Evans
H 9/20	New York	4	Chicago	2	Schupp	Lavender
H /9/21	New York	4	Chicago	0	Perritt	Hendrix
H 9/22	New York	5	Chicago	0	Sallee	Perry
H 9/23	New York	6	St. Louis	1	Tesreau	Watson
H 9/23	New York	3	St. Louis	0	Benton	Ames
H 9/25	New York	1	St. Louis	0	Schupp	Meadows
H 9/25	New York	6	St. Louis	2	Perritt	Lotz
H 9/26	New York	6	St. Louis	1	Sallee	Watson
H 9/27	New York	3	St. Louis	2	Ritter	Steele
H 9/28	New York	2	Boston	0	Tesreau	Rudolph
H 9/28	New York	6	Boston	0	Schupp	Ragan
H 9/30	New York	4	Boston	0	Benton	Rudolph

9/30/16 second game doubleheader lost to Boston 8-3 WP Tyler LB Sallee

1935 Chicago Cub Winning Streak

H 9/4	Chicago	8	Philadelphia	2
H 9/5	Chicago	3	Philadelphia	2
H 9/6	Chicago	3	Philadelphia	2
H 9/7	Chicago	4	Philadelphia	0
H 9/9	Chicago	5	Boston	1
H 9/9	Chicago	2	Boston	1
H 9/10	Chicago	4	Boston	0
H 9/11	Chicago	15	Boston	3
H 9/12	Chicago	13	Brooklyn	3
H 9/13	Chicago	4	Brooklyn	1
H 9/14	Chicago	18	Brooklyn	14
H 9/15	Chicago	6	Brooklyn	3
H 9/16	Chicago	8	New York	3
H 9/17	Chicago	5	New York	3
H 9/18	Chicago	15	New York	3
H 9/19	Chicago	6	New York	1
H 9/21	Chicago	4	Pittsburgh	3
H 9/22	Chicago	2	Pittsburgh	0
A 9/25	Chicago	1	St. Louis	0
	Warneke beats P. Dean			
A 9/27	Chicago	6	St. Louis	2
A 9/27	Chicago	5	St. Louis	3

Streak began after Chicago lost second game of doubleheader at home to Cincinnati four to two on 9/2/35. Streak ended on 9/28/35 at St. Louis when Cardinals won seven to five.

Oakland A's 2002 Twenty Game Win Streak

H 8/13	Toronto	5-4	Zito	Carpenter
H 8/14	Toronto	4-2	Hudson	Walker
H 8/16	Chicago	1-0	Lidle	Buehrle
H 8/17	Chicago	9-2	Mulder	Garland
H 8/18	Chicago	7-4	Zito	Wright
A 8/19	Cleveland	8-1	Hudson	Baez
A 8/20	Cleveland	6-3	Harrang	Westbrook
A 8/21	Cleveland	6-0	Lidle	Rodriguez
A 8/22	Cleveland	9-3	Mulder	Phillips
A 8/23	Detroit	9-1	Zito	Powell

A 8/24	Detroit	12-3	Hudson	Lima
A 8/25	Detroit	10-7	Mecir	Walker
A 8/26	KC	6-3	Lidle	May
A 8/27	KC	6-4	Mulder	Hernandez
A 8/28	KC	7-1	Zito	Sedlacek
H 8/30	Minnesota	4-2	Hudson	Radke
H 8/31	Minnesota	6-3	Mecir	Romero
H 9/1	Minnesota	7-5	Koch	Guardado
H 9/2	KC	7-6	Koch	Grimsley
H 9/4	KC	12-11	Koch	Grimsley

Streak ended at Minnesota when Twins defeat A's six to zero Radke beats Lidle

Losing Streaks

As long as baseball has been organized, the glamour of the winning streak always brings glory to those teams. At the other end of the spectrum, a prolonged losing streak will create ridicule that will endure through the ages. The perfect example of this would be the Cleveland Spiders of 1899, who had the worst won-lost record of all time (20-134) that included a twenty-four game losing streak. However, this not the longest in history.

Listed are the teams who had twenty or more losses in a row. The first on the list are the 1889 Louisville of the American Association who went twenty-six consecutive games without tasting victory.

Louisville 1889 AA Twenty-Six Game Losing Streak

H 5/22	Baltimore	11-2	Cunningham	Ewing
H 5/23	Baltimore	9-8	Kilroy	Ehret
H 5/26	Cincinnati	16-4	Duryea	Ehret
A 5/27	Cincinnati	10-9	Viau Started - Smith won relief Stratton	
A 5/28	Cincinnati	13-12	Mullane	Ehret
A 5/31	Colorado	7-2	Baldwin	Stratton
A 6/1	Colorado	8-3	Widner	Ramsey
A 6/2	Colorado	11-4	Baldwin	Ewing
A 6/3	Colorado	12-3	Mays	Ehret
A 6/5	Philadelphia	11-10	Weyhing	Stratton
A 6/6	Philadelphia	5-2	Seward	Tomney
A 6/6	Philadelphia	16-3	Coleman	Ehret

41

A 6/7 Philadelphia 9-7   Knouff   Ramsey
(Game played for benefit of Johnstown flood sufferers)
A 6/8 Brooklyn   14-5   Caruthers   Stratton
A 6/9 Brooklyn   12-2   Lovett   Ramsey
A 6/10 Brooklyn   7-5   Caruthers
A 6/11 Brooklyn   4-2   Lovett   Ramsey
A 6/13 Baltimore   4-2   Cunningham Ehret
                          Five inning stopped rain
A 6/15 Baltimore   4-2   Kilroy   Ramsey
A 6/17 Baltimore   10-6   Goetz   Ramsey
A 6/17 Baltimore   10-0   Forman   Ehret
One hitter by Baltimore pitcher no-hitter broken up by Louisville's Farmer Weaver

Cleveland 1899 National League Twenty-Four Game Losing Streak

8/26 New York   2-1   Doheny   Schmit
                Called after 5 innings, wet grounds
8/28 Boston   6-4   Willis   Hughey
8/29 Boston   11-3   Klobedanz   Colliflower
8/29 Boston   9-1   Nichols   Knepper
8/30 Boston   8-5   Lewis   Bates
8/31 Brooklyn   9-3   Hughes   Schmit
9/1   Brooklyn   7-2   Dunn   Hughey
9/1   Brooklyn   5-1   McJames   Colliflower
9/3   Cincinnati   3-1   Breitenstein Knepper
9/4   Cincinnati   6-3   Hawley   Hughey
9/4   Cincinnati   8-1   Taylor   Schmit
9/5   Cincinnati   19-3   Phillips   Bates
9/5   Cincinnati   9-7   Frisk   Colliflower
9/7   Chicago   7-6   Taylor   Knepper
           (Chicago scores 3 runs in bottom of 9th)
9/8   Chicago   5-1   Griffith   Hughey
9/9   Chicago   5-2   Callahan   Schmit
9/9   Chicago   11-0   Garvin   Bates
9/10 Cincinnati   10-2   Frisk   Colliflower
9/12 Philadelphia 11-0   Orth   Knepper
9/12 Philadelphia 8-4   Piatt   Schmit
9/13 Philadelphia 8-2   Donahue   Wilson

42

9/14	Philadelphia	8-0	Bernhard	Hughey
9/15	Washington	14-3	Evans	Schmit
9/16	Washington	15-10	Fifield	Knepper

(Cleveland blows 8-1 leads from second inning on)

This streak was broken 5-4 vs. Washington on 9/18 - Cleveland scores in bottom of tenth WP Harder   LP McGee

Philadelphia 1961 National League Twenty-Three game losing streak

7/29	San Francisco	4-3	McCormick	Ferrarese
7/30	San Francisco	5-2	Sanford	Owen

7/31 Eighty-one All Star Game

8/2	Cincinnati	4-2	O'Toole	Mahaffey
8/2	Cincinnati	3-2	Jay	Short
8/3	Cincinnati	7-1	Johnson	Buzhardt
8/4	St. Louis	9-8	Bruligio	Ferrarese
8/5	St. Louis	7-0	Simmons	Brown
8/6	St. Louis	3-1	Sadecki	Sullivan
8/6	St. Louis	3-2	Gibson	Owens
8/7	Pittsburgh	3-1	Friend	Buzhardt
8/8	Pittsburgh	10-2	Haddix	Mahaffey
8/8	Pittsburgh	3-2	Sturdivant	Short
8/9	Cincinnati	5-0	Jay	Ferrarese
8/11	Pittsburgh	6-0	Friend	Roberts

Game called rain

8/12	Pittsburgh	4-0	Mivell	Owens
8/13	Pittsburgh	13-4	Stundivant	Buzhardt
8/14	Chicago	9-2	Ellsworth	Sullivan
8/15	Chicago	6-5	Curtis	Mahaffey
8/16	Chicago	9-5	Caldwell	Short
8/17	Milwaukee	7-6	Huttenbart	Ballsham

Boone scores in bottom 11th for 20th loss

8/18	Milwaukee	4-1	Burdette	Owens
8/19	Milwaukee	4-3	Cloninger	Sullivan
8/20	Milwaukee	5-2	Spahn	Short First game of

D.H.

Streak ends on 8/20 in the second game of double-header vs. Milwaukee.

Final score: Philadelphia seven, Milwaukee four, Buzhardt beats Willey.

Pittsburgh 1890 Twenty-Three game losing streak

A 8/9	Chicago	7-4	Luby	Osborne	1st game
H 8/12	Chicago	13-12	Hutchinson	Gumbert	12 Innings
A 8/13	Cleveland	20-9	Young	Osborne	
A 8/14	Cleveland	11-6	Beatin	Phillips	
A 8/15	Cleveland	15-0	Beatin	Gary	
A 8/16	Chicago	18-5	Hutchinson	Phillips	
A 8/18	Chicago	9-3	Stein	Hecker	
A 8/19	Chicago	18-3	Hutchinson	Hayner	2nd game
A 8/21	Philadelphia	7-4	Vickery	Heard	
A 8/22	Philadelphia	12-0	Gleason	Osborne	
A 8/23	Philadelphia	7-0	J. Smith	Esper	
A 8/25	Boston	15-2	Clarkson	Phillips	
A 8/26	Boston	10-3	Nichols	Heard	
A 8/27	Boston	16-7	Clarkson	Osborn	
A 8/27	New York	11-3	Getlein	Phillips	
A 8/28	New York	9-1	Sharrot	Esper	
A 8/30	New York	1-0	Welch	Anderson	
A 8/30	New York	5-0	Rusie	Phillips	
A 8/30	New York	7-3	Sharrot	Heard	
A 9/1	Brooklyn	10-9	Caruthers	Baker	
A 9/1	Brooklyn	3-2	Lovett	Anderson	
A 9/1	Brooklyn	8-4	Terry	Anderson	
A 9/2	Brooklyn	5-4	Caruthers	Day	

Brooklyn scores 3 in top of the 9th to win.

This streak ended 9/3/90 when Pittsburgh scores four in ninth - three on Kelty HR with Pittsburgh winning eleven to ten over Philadelphia

Philadelphia American Association in 1890
Twenty-Two Game Losing Streak

A 9/16	Baltimore	5-1	German	Green
A 9/19	Louisville	9-4	Meakim	O'Neil
A 9/20	Louisville	22-4	Stratton	Green
A 9/20	Louisville	10-0	Ehret	Stecher
A 9/21	Louisville	12-4	Goodall	O'Neil

44

A 9/21	Louisville	16-3	Daily	Stecher
A 9/23	St. Louis	21-2	Nicol	Green
A 9/26	St. Louis	15-3	Neale	Green
A 9/26	St. Louis	7-3	Nicol	Stecher
A 9/27	Toledo	15-3	Sprague	O'Neil
A 9/28	Toledo	11-9	Cushman	Stecher
A 9/30	Columbus	14-3	Easton	O'Neil
A 10/1	Columbus	14-0	Knauss	Stecher
A 10/2	Columbus	10-2	Gastright	Green
A 10/4	Syracuse	7-6	Casey	O'Neil
A 10/4	Syracuse	6-1	Mars	Green
H 10/8	Rochester	17-1	Barr	O'Neil
H 10/9	Rochester	10-4	Fields	Stecher
H 10/11	Syracuse	16-1	Mars	Green
H 10/11	Syracuse	15-4	Keefe	Helmbold
H 10/12	Syracuse	12-2	Mars	Sterling

Louisville Twenty Game Losing Streak National League 1894

A 5/28	Pittsburgh	4-2	Gumbert	Menefee
A 5/28	Pittsburgh	11-6	Killen	Kilroy
A 5/29	Washington	12-2	Mercer	Hemming
A 5/30	Washington	7-3	Petty	Knell
A 6/1	Pittsburgh	10-3	Taylor	Menefee

Philadelphia scored seven in twelfth to win

A 6/2	Philadelphia	11-0	Weyhing	Hemming
A 6/4	Brooklyn	18-4	Daub	Knell
A 6/5	Brooklyn	5-4	Kennedy	Menefee
A 6/7	Baltimore	7-5	Inks	Hemming
A 6/8	Baltimore	14-2	Hawke	Stratton
A 6/9	Baltimore	7-5	McMahon	Knell
A 6/11	New York	8-3	Rusie	Hemming
A 6/12	New York	4-1	Meekin	Stratton
A 6/13	New York	7-5	Rusie	Hemming
A 6/14	Boston	9-6	Staley	Knell
A 6/15	Boston	15-10	Stivetts	Stratton
A 6/16	Boston	16-10	Lovett	Stratton
A 6/18	Pittsburgh	9-8	Colcolough	Knell
A 6/18	Pittsburgh	11-1	Killen	Knell

Streak Broken 6/19 Lou Beats Pittsburgh nine to four at Pittsburgh
Hemming beats Easton

Boston American League 1906 Losing Streak

A 5/1	New York	8-0	Hogg	Gibson
H 5/2	Washington	3-2	Patten	Young
H 5/3	Washington	6-4	Kitson	Winter
H 5/4	Washington	4-2	Hughes	Dinneen
H 5/7	Philadelphia	4-0	Waddell	Winter
H 5/8	Pittsburgh	11-4	Coakley	Tannehill
H 5/9	Pittsburgh	9-5	Plank	Young
H 5/10	Philadelphia	5-1	Bender	Harris
H 5/11	St. Louis	8-3	Smith	Dinneen
H 5/12	St. Louis	9-1	Glade	Gibson
H 5/14	St. Louis	11-1	Howell	Young
H 5/16	Cleveland	7-6	Rhodes	Winter
H 5/17	Cleveland	7-4	Hess	Harris
H 5/18	Cleveland	14-1	Joss	Dinneen
H 5/19	Cleveland	3-2	Bernhard	Young
H 5/21	Detroit	2-1	Mullin	Winter
H 5/22	Detroit	6-3	Siever	Harris
H 5/23	Detroit	3-2	Killian	Dinneen
H 5/24	Chicago	7-5	Altrock	Young

Streak ends when Boston defeats Chicago three to zero on 5/25 Tannehill
beats White

Philadelphia American League 1916 Losing Streak

H 7/21	Cleveland	7-2	Coumbe	Nabors
A 7/25	St. Louis	8-3	Koob	Lanning
A 7/26	St. Louis	5-1	Davenport	Bush
A 7/27	St. Louis	3-2	Hamilton	Nabors
A 7/28	St. Louis	8-6	Groom	Sheehan
A 7/29	Chicago	6-1	Faber	Myers
A 7/29	Chicago	6-4	Benz	Bush
A 7/30	Chicago	10-1	Cicotte	Lanning
A 7/31	Chicago	4-3	Sheehan	Faber
A 8/1	Chicago	3-0	Russell	Nabors
A 8/2	Chicago	8-2	Benz	Williams

A 8/3	Cleveland	3-1	Bagby	Bush
A 8/4	Cleveland	5-2	Beebe	Sheehan
A 8/5	Cleveland	2-3	Coveleski	Johnson

1943 Philadelphia A's Losing Streak

H 8/7	New York	3-1	Wensloff	Black
H 8/8	New York	7-1	Chandler	Harris
H 8/9	New York	8-4	Murphy	Wolff
A 8/11	Cleveland	10-5	Reynolds	Ciola
A 8/12	Cleveland	4-3	Bagby	Arntzen
A 8/13	Cleveland	6-4	Harder	Black
A 8/14	Cleveland	12-9	Dean	Fagan
A 8/15	Detroit	5-4	Trout	Harris
A 8/15	Detroit	3-2	Bridges	Wolff
A 8/16	Detroit	4-3	Trout	Flores
A 8/18	St. Louis	4-0	Muncrief	Arntzen
A 8/19	St. Louis	3-0	Galehouse	Black
A 8/21	St. Louis	5-3	Sundra	Harris
A 8/21	St. Louis	4-1	Newsom	Wolff
A 8/22	Chicago	5-2	Smith	Mains
A 5/22	Chicago	3-2	Humphries	Flores
A 8/23	Chicago	7-6	Maltzberger	Ciola
A 8/23	Chicago	7-0	Grove	Black
A 8/24	Chicago	6-5	Ross	Harris

8/24 Streak ends - second game of double-header, Pittsburgh eight, Chicago one, Wolff beats Dietrich

1969 Montreal Losing Streak

			WP	LP
H 5/13	Houston	10-3	Billingham	McGinn
H 5/14	Houston	3-1	Lemaster	Grant
H 5/16	Atlanta	7-5	Raymond	Face
H 5/18	Atlanta	8-3	Reed	Wegner
A 5/20	Houston	5-0	Dierker	Grant
A 5/21	Houston	3-2	Lemaster	Stoneman
A 5/22	Houston	7-4	Wilson	Jaster
A 5/23	Cincinnati	4-3	Carroll	McGinn
A 5/24	Cincinnati	11-2	Cloninger	Grant

A 5/25	Cincinnati	7-2	Merritt	Stoneman
H 5/27	Los Angeles	5-3	Singer	McGinn
H 5/28	Los Angeles	6-0	Sutton	Robertson
H 5/29	Los Angeles	5-3	Osteen	Stoneman
H 5/30	San Diego	3-2	Baldschun	McGinn
H 5/31	San Diego	6-2	Niekro	Jaster
H 6/1	San Diego	5-2	Podres	Robertson
H 6/3	San Francisco	9-3	Sadecki	Stoneman
H 6/4	San Francisco	8-3	McCormick	Wegener
A 6/6	Los Angeles	4-2	Sutton	McGinn
A 6/7	Los Angeles	9-5	Osteen	Stoneman

6/8 broke streak at Los Angeles - beat Dodgers four to three, Robertson defeated Singer

1988 Baltimore Twenty-One Game Losing Streak

H 4/4	Milwaukee	12-0	Higuera	Boddicker
H 4/6	Milwaukee	3-1	Bosio	Morgan
A 4/8	Cleveland	3-0	Bailes	Thurmond
A 4/9	Cleveland	21-1	Candiotti	Boddicker
A 4/10	Cleveland	6-3	Yett	McGregor
A 4/11	Cleveland	7-2	Swindell	Morgan
H 4/12	KC	6-1	Gubicza	Peraza
H 4/13	KC	9-3	Bannister	Thurmond
H 4/14	KC	3-2	Yett	McGregor
H 4/16	Cleveland	1-0	Swindell	Schmidt 11 innings
H 4/17	Cleveland	4-1	Farrell	Peraza
A 4/19	Milwaukee	9-5	Nieves	Thurmond
A 4/20	Milwaukee	8-6	Wegman	Boddicker
A 4/21	Milwaukee	7-1	Bosio	McGregor
A 4/22	KC	13-1	Gubicza	Morgan
A 4/23	KC	4-3	Power	Sisk
A 4/24	KC	3-1	Saberhagen	Thurmond
A 4/26	Minnesota	4-2	Viola	Morgan
A 4/27	Minnesota	7-6	Berenguer	Scherrer
A 4/28	Minnesota	4-2	Anderson	Boddicker

An away game 4/29, they broke the streak nine to zero, Chicago White Sox Williamson defeats McDowell

Teams Same City with Both Teams Losing One Hundred Games the Same Year

It's bad when a city has one of its teams lose one hundred or more games in a year. But when both entities hit the century mark there cannot be any relief of frustration for any of the fans. This scenario happened four times in the game's history. See below for the unhappy outcomes.

1906 Boston America League 49-105
     Boston National League 49-102

1921 Philadelphia America League 53-100
     Philadelphia National League 51-103

1936 Philadelphia America League 53-100
     Philadelphia National League 54-100

1940 Philadelphia American League 54-100
     Philadelphia National League 50-103

Teams Same City with Both Teams Winning One Hundred Games the Same Year

The city of New York witnessed the joy of having two of their three teams hit the one hundred mark or more in the same year. Only one of the two years was a subway series played.

1941 New York American League 101-53
     Brooklyn National League   100-54

1942 New York American League 103-51
     Brooklyn National League   104-50 * Finished second to St. Louis

The 250 Hit Men

Only six times in the history of the game has anyone made 250 or more hits in a season. In 1920, George Sisler of the St. Louis Browns not only broke the 250 hit barrier, but also set the all-time record. Bill Terry and Chuck Klein were the last to hit that mark. Terry tied the National League record set the previous year by Lefty O'Doul. Klein, by the way, is the only man with 250 hits not to lead the league in hits. Another bit of information is that Klein and O'Doul are the only teammates that have made 250 or more hits in a season. In 2001, Ichiro Suzuki had the highest total since 1930, with 242. It shows you how difficult the feat is to accomplish. The sixth time that it was done was in the 154 game schedule.

250 Hits in a Season
American League

| G. Sisler | St. Louis | 1920 | 257 |
| A. Simmons | Philadelphia | 1925 | 253 |

National League

R. Hornsby	St. Louis	1922	250
L. O'Doul	Philadelphia	1929	254
B. Terry	New York	1930	254
C. Klein	Philadelphia	1930	250

Batters with Less Than Ten Strikeouts a Season Greater or Equal one hundred Games and Greater or Equal Four Hundred AB

Since the leagues started keeping record of batters' strikeouts (the National League in1910 and the American League in 1913), there have been only thirty-three times that batters finished under ten strikeouts in a season. Since the arrival of the home run game, the increase in batters' strikeouts increased significantly. The last time anyone had less than ten K's in the American League was Dale Mitchell in 1952. This is the same batter who ended Larsen's perfect game in the World Series with a strikeout. The last time anyone had less than ten strikeouts in the senior circuit was Don Mueller in 1956.

American League

1918	T. Speaker	Cleveland	9
1921	H. Severeid	St. Louis	9
1922	S. McInnis	Cleveland	5
1923	E. Collins	Chicago	8

1925	J. Sewell	Cleveland	4
1926	J. Sewell	Cleveland	6
1926	H. Summa	Cleveland	9
1927	J. Sewell	Cleveland	7
1927	M. Cochrane	Philadelphia	7
1927	T. Speaker	Washington	8
1928	J. Sewell	Cleveland	9
1929	J. Sewell	Cleveland	4
1929	M. Cochrane	Philadelphia	8
1929	S. Rice	Washington	9
1930	J. Sewell	Cleveland	3
1931	J. Sewell	New York	8
1932	J. Sewell	New York	3
1933	J. Sewell	New York	4
1945	E. Bush	Philadelphia	9
1948	L. Boudreau	Cleveland	9
1952	D. Mitchell	Cleveland	9

National League

1921	E. Roush	Cincinnati	8
1921	C. Deal	Chicago	9
1922	C. Hollocher	Chicago	5
1924	S. McInnis	Boston	6
1926	A. High	Boston	9
1929	P. Traynor	Pittsburgh	7
1931	F. Leach	New York	9
1933	L. Waner	Pittsburgh	8
1936	L. Waner	Pittsburgh	5
1945	T. Holmes	Boston	9
1947	E. Verban	Philadelphia	8
1956	D. Mueller	New York	7

Joe Sewell: The Master of Contact

In 1920, Joe Sewell was rushed to the major leagues by the Cleveland Indians because of the death of Ray Chapman. Carl Mays of the New York Yankees beaned Chapman. Chapman died the following day and the Indians, fighting to win their first pennant, needed an immediate replacement. Sewell was their selection. He established himself quickly as a hitter who did not strikeout. Throughout his career, he was usually over the .300 mark, which can be attested by his .312 lifetime average. Not a power hitter, Sewell's forte was making contact. In his career, he struck out only 114 times over a fourteen-year period. Nine times he finished under ten times. From 1925 to 1933, his last year, he whiffed an unbelievable forty-eight times. In four years, he had four or less strikeouts for the season.

His one hundred fourteen-career total is less than any American League strikeout leader since 1958.

 In the National League, his career total is less than the league strikeout leader since 1960, excluding the strikes of 1981 and 1994.

Joe Sewell Strikeout

Year	Team	G	AB	H	K	BA	K/AB	K/G
1920	Cleveland	22	70	23	4	.329	17.5	5.5
1921	Cleveland	154	572	182	17	.318	33.6	9.1
1922	Cleveland	153	558	187	20	.299	27.9	7.7
1923	Cleveland	153	553	195	12	.353	46.1	11.8
1924	Cleveland	153	594	188	13	.318	45.7	12.8
1925	Cleveland	155	608	204	4	.336	152.0	38.8
1926	Cleveland	154	578	187	6	.324	96.3	25.7
1927	Cleveland	153	569	180	7	.316	86.3	21.9
1928	Cleveland	155	588	190	9	.323	65.3	19.2
1929	Cleveland	152	578	182	4	.315	144.5	38.0
1930	Cleveland	109	353	102	3	.289	17.7	36.3
1931	New York	130	484	146	8	.302	60.5	16.3
1932	New York	125	503	137	3	.272	167.7	41.7
1933	New York	135	524	138	4	.273	131.0	33.8

*National Sports Encyclopedia baseball error - 1926, has seven. It should be listed as six. Lifetime totals should be one hundred fourteen up in the book.

Men with One Hundred Extra Base Hits in a Season

Before 2001, there were only eight men who accumulated one hundred extra base hits in a season. In 2001, the list grew fifty percent due to the surge in power hitting. Not only did Barry Bonds set a new homer mark by hitting seventy-three homers, he became only the second man to top a slugging percentage of .800. He erased Babe Ruth's record of .847 and replaced it with his own of .863. He also tied Chuck Klein's National League record of one hundred seven extra base hits in a season. Three others joined Bonds with one hundred or more extra base hits. Two of them had fifty plus homers, with the fourth just missing the fifty-mark by one. Also it was the first time in National League history two men topped a .700 slugging average in a year.

American League

			2B	3B	HR	Total
B. Ruth	New York	1921	44	16	59	119
L. Gehrig	New York	1927	52	18	47	117
J. Foxx	Philadelphia	1932	33	9	58	100
A. Belle	Cleveland	1995	52	1	50	103

National League

			2B	3B	HR	Total
R. Hornsby	St. Louis	1922	46	14	42	102
C. Klein	Philadelphia	1930	59	8	40	107
C. Klein	Philadelphia	1932	50	15	38	103
S. Musial	St. Louis	1948	46	18	39	103
B. Bonds	San Francisco	2001	32	2	73	107
T. Helton	Colorado	2001	54	2	49	105
S. Sosa	Chicago	2001	34	5	64	103
L. Gonzalez	Arizona	2001	36	7	57	100

Teammates with Twenty or More Triples in the Same Year

It's rare when one player on a team gathers twenty or more triples but when two do it on the same team in the same year it is an extreme rarity. It has been accomplished only three times in baseball history.

American League				National League			
B. Keister	Baltimore	1901	21	D. Wilson Pittsburgh		1912	36
J. Williams	Baltimore	1901	21	H. Wagner Pittsburgh		1912	30
T. Cobb	Detroit	1912	23				
J. Crawford	Detroit	1912	21				

Teammates with Fifty or More Doubles in the Same Year.

It was once a rarity when someone got fifty plus doubles in a year. Today the league leader in that category is frequently achieving fifty or more. In the National League, the leader has had fifty or more during the last seven years. The American League leader has accomplished fifty or more six out of the last nine years. What is an extreme accomplishment is when two teammates hit that mark in the same year. That has only happened three times all in the American League.

H. Greenberg	Detroit	1934	63
C. Gehringer	Detroit	1934	50
C. Gehringer	Detroit	1936	60
G. Walker	Detroit	1936	55
M. Vernon	Washington	1946	51
S. Spence	Washington	1946	50

The All .400 Hitting Outfield

It is a managers delight to have an all .300 hitting outfield. It has happened a myriad of times. What is the rarest of all baseball exploits occurred in 1894. The only time that a team had it three outfielders top the .400 mark in batting was the Philadelphia Phillies. They had Sam Thompson, Ed Delahanty and Billy Hamilton achieve .400 plus average. The irony of the season was none of the three won the batting title and the Phils did not win the pennant.

E. Delahanty		B. Hamilton		S. Thompsom	
1894	.404	1894	.403	1894	.415
1895	.404				
1899	.410				

Ed Delahanty	.404
Billy Hamilton	.403
Sam Thompson	.415

The Triple Twenties:
Hitters with Twenty or More Doubles, Triples and Homers

This is another area that has a short list of achievers. Only five times has it happened, with George Brett in 1979, being the last. Oddly, the first time it was done was during the dead ball era. In 1911, Frank Schulte of the Chicago Cubs somehow muscled twenty-one homers, a huge amount during this time. This coincided with his thirty doubles and twenty-one triples. This display of power earned "Wildfire" the National Leagues first Chalmers Award. That was equivalent to today's MVP award.

American League		**2B**	**3B**	**HR**
1941 J. Heath	Cleveland	32	20	24
1979 G. Brett	KC	42	20	23

National League		**2B**	**3B**	**HR**
1911 F. Schulte	Chicago	30	21	21
1928 J. Bottomley	St. Louis	42	20	31
1957 W. Mays	New York	26	20	35

Leading League in RBI's Three Consecutive Years

This is another abbreviated list with some surprising names on it. Only six times has this occurred with the usual names of Ruth and Hornsby appearing. The last two accomplishers will raise some eyebrows, but they did it.

American League
Ty Cobb	Detroit	1907-1909
Babe Ruth	Boston/New York	1919-1921
Cecil Fielder	Detroit	1990-1992

National League
| Honus Wagner | Pittsburgh | 1907-1909 |
| Rogers Hornsby | St. Louis | 1920-1922 |

George Foster   Cincinnati   1976-1978

Batters with 3000 Hits and 400 Home Runs

Only seven men can place their names in this group. All of the seven have plaques on the wall of the Hall of Fame. If you take the first three names in alphabetical order, the list would shrink to just those three if you only include 3000 hits and 500 home runs.

	Hits	**Home Runs**
H. Aaron	3771	755
W. Mays	3283	660
E. Murray	3253	504
S. Musial	3630	475
C. Ripken	3184	431
D. Winfield	3110	465
C. Yastrzemski	3419	452

The .700 Slugging Averages

In 1920, Babe Ruth not only broke the .700 mark in slugging but also broke the .800 mark. The following year he topped .800 again, finishing .001 below his 1920 percentage. No one including Ruth would see .800 until Barry Bonds bested Ruth, what was thought unattainable, in 2001 at .863. These two are the only ones to surpass .800 slugging. In regard to the .700 average, Ruth at the height of his career broke the .700 percentage nine times. The only others who had repeated that mark were Lou Gehrig, Jimmy Foxx and Ted Williams. Gehrig and Foxx did it three times while "the Splendid Splinter" achieved it twice. Two of the three times that Gehrig hit the mark he was runner up to Ruth. These are the only two times that teammates had .700 slugging averages the same year. It shows you how potent the Yankee offense was with Ruth and Gehrig in the same batting order. In the American League, the .700 was surpassed twenty-two times. This seems like a lot but it is not. When you break it down Ruth did it nine times with Gehrig and Foxx accounting for six of these times. Ted Williams name also appears twice. Those four players amassed seventeen of the twenty-two successes at the .700 target, which left five others who topped the mark.

In the National League, Barry Bonds' assault of the number has happened the past three years with one setting the all-time record of .863. He joined Roger Hornsby and Larry Walker as the only senior circuit sluggers to have multiple .700 slugging averages. In fact, when Bonds set the all-time slugging mark he was joined by Sammy Sosa who came in second in 2001 with a .737, the only time two National Leagues did it in the same year.

American League

B. Ruth	New York	1920	.847	L. Gehrig	New York	1927	.765
B. Ruth	New York	1921	.846	L. Gehrig	New York	1930	.721
B. Ruth	New York	1923	.764	L. Gehrig	New York	1934	.706
B. Ruth	New York	1924	.739				
B. Ruth	New York	1926	.737	J. Foxx	Philadelphia	1932	.749
B. Ruth	New York	1927	.772	J. Foxx	Philadelphia	1933	.703
B. Ruth	New York	1928	.709	J. Foxx	Philadelphia	1938	.704
B. Ruth	New York	1930	.732				
B. Ruth	New York	1931	.700	T. Williams	Boston	1941	.735
				T. Williams	Boston	1957	.731

A. Simmons	Philadelphia	1930	.708
M. Mantle	New York	1956	.705
F. Thomas	Chicago	1994	.729
A. Belle	Cleveland	1994	.714
M. McGwire	Oakland	1996	.730

National League

R. Hornsby	St. Louis	1922	.722	L. Walker	Colorado	1997	.720
R. Hornsby	St. Louis	1925	.756	L. Walker	Colorado	1999	.710
H. Wilson	Chicago	1930	.723	M. McGwire	St. Louis	1998	.752
S. Musial	St. Louis	1948	.702	S. Sosa	Chicago	2001	.737
J. Bagwell	Houston	1994	.750				

B. Bonds	San Francisco	2001	.863
B. Bonds	San Francisco	2002	.799
B. Bonds	San Francisco	2003	.749

Facts about Slugging Percentage

The only teammates to slug .700 or better the same year:

1927 New York   B. Ruth .772   L. Gehrig .721
1930 New York   B. Ruth .732   L. Gehrig .721

The most batters to slug .700 in a season:

3-1930 American League	B. Ruth	.732
	L. Gehrig	.721
	A. Simmons	.708

2-2001 National League	B. Bonds	.863
	S. Sosa	.737

The only men to slug .700 with two different teams:

American League
J. Foxx   Philadelphia 1932 & 1933
         Boston 1938

Both leagues:
M. McGwire   American League   Oakland   1996
             National League   St. Louis   1998

Only men to slug .700 and not lead the league:

American League		National League	
L. Gehrig	1927	S. Sosa	2001
L. Gehrig	1930		
A. Simmons	1930		
A. Belle	1994		

The Four Hundred Total Base Men

In 2001, four men hit one hundred extra base hits (Sosa, Bonds, Gonzalez and Helton) also achieved another difficult goal. This was amassing four hundred or more total bases in a season, which has been attained twenty-nine times in both leagues. This does not seem so difficult but it is because only eighteen men through the years did it. In the American League, only once has it been reached since 1937, and that was by Jim Rice in 1978. In 1997, the National League had its first batter do it since 1959, when Hank Aaron did it with exactly Four hundred TB's. Since Aaron, it has been done seven times.

American League

1921	B. Ruth	New York	457
1927	L. Gehrig	New York	447
1927	B. Ruth	New York	417
1930	L. Gehrig	New York	419
1931	L. Gehrig	New York	410
1932	J. Foxx	Philadelphia	438
1933	J. Foxx	Philadelphia	403
1934	L. Gehrig	New York	409
1936	H. Trosky	Cleveland	405
1936	L. Gehrig	New York	403
1937	J. DiMaggio	New York	418
1978	J. Rice	Boston	406

National League

1922	R. Hornsby	St. Louis	450
1929	R. Hornsby	Chicago	409
1929	C. Klein	Philadelphia	405
1930	C. Klein	Philadelphia	445
1930	H. Wilson	Chicago	423
1930	B. Herman	Brooklyn	416
1932	C. Klein	Philadelphia	420
1937	J. Medwick	St. Louis	406
1948	S. Musial	St. Louis	429
1959	H. Aaron	Milwaukee	400
1997	L. Walker	Colorado	405
1998	S. Sosa	Chicago	425
2001	L. Gonzalez	Arizona	419
2001	B. Bonds	San Francisco	411
2001	T. Helton	Colorado	402

Facts on Four Hundred Total Bases

Only two men have hit for 450 TB's and they are Babe Ruth with 457 and Rogers Hornsby with 450.

Only two men have done it more than twice and they are Lou Gehrig and Chuck Klein.

Only four men did it in consecutive years.

Lou Gehrig   1930 and 1931
C. Klein   1929 and 1930
Jimmy Foxx   1932 and 1933
Todd Helton   2000 and 2001

Only once did teammates do it in the same year, Babe Ruth and Lou Gehringer in 1927.

Rogers Hornsby did and was the only man to it for two different teams, St. Louis in 1922, and Chicago in 1929.

The One Hundred Fifty Run Scorers in a Season

Jeff Bagwell ended the twentieth century doing something that had not been accomplished in fifty-one years. He was the first man to score one hundred fifty or more runs in a season, when Ted Williams did it in 1949. In fact, it has been sixty-eight years since any National Leaguer dented the plate that many times, when Chuck Klein scored one hundred fifty-two runs in 1932. The feat has been done eleven times in the American League and seven times in the National League.

American League

1920	B. Ruth	New York	158
1929	R. Hornsby	Chicago	156
1923	B. Ruth	New York	151
1929	L. O'Doul	Philly	152
1927	B. Ruth	New York	158
1930	C. Klein	Philadelphia	158
1928	B. Ruth	New York	163
1930	K. Cuyler	Chicago	155
1930	A. Simmons	Philadelphia	152
1930	W. English	Chicago	152
1930	B. Ruth	New York	150

1932	C. Klein	Philadelphia	152
1931	L. Gehrig	New York	163
2000	J. Bagwell	Houston	152
1932	J. Foxx	Philadelphia	151
1936	L. Gehrig	New York	167
1937	J. DiMaggio	New York	151
1949	T. Williams	Boston	150

Facts About One Hundred Fifty Run Scores

The only men to score one hundred fifty or more runs and not lead the league in scoring.

American League	B. Ruth	New York	1930
National League	K. Cuyler	Chicago	1930
	W. English	Chicago	1930

The only teammates that scored one hundred fifty or more runs in a season was National Leaguers K. Cuyler and W. English of the Chicago Cubs.

Men with One Hundred Fifty RBI's in a Season

This has happened forty-one times during baseball's history. One might ask the question "What is so unique about that?" The answer to this is, thirty of those times occurred before 1940. The power explosion due to the lively ball during the 1920's and 1930's was dominated by a handful of batters. From 1940 on, the one hundred fifty RBI plateau was only reached eleven times in a period of sixty-five years.

When Joe Medwick won his triple crown in 1937 (with one hundred fifty-four RBI's), it took another twenty-five years before another National Leaguer would be able to reach the one hundred fifty mark. From 1962 to 1996, would be the next time the 150 levels would be obtained. Since 1996, one man, Sammy Sosa, has reached the goal twice.

In the American League, one hundred fifty was topped by teammates Ted Williams and Vern Stephens in 1949, both with one hundred fifty-nine. It would be forty-nine years later that the next American Leaguer would see one hundred fifty or more RBI's. Juan Gonzalez and Albert Belle would crack the ceiling.

So regardless of the amount of times one hundred fifty were reached, the fact of the matter is that one twenty-year period dominated the statistical goal. Close to one-half of the twentieth century elapsed before an American Leaguer obtained the goal. In the National League only once in a six decade period was 150 RBI's amassed.

American League

L. Gehrig			B. Ruth		
1927 New York	175		1921 New York	171	
1930 New York	174		1927 New York	164	
1931 New York	184		1929 New York	154	
1932 New York	151		1930 New York	153	
1934 New York	165		1931 New York	163	
1936 New York	152				
1937 New York	159				

J. Foxx			A. Simmons		
1930 Philadelphia	156		1929 Philadelphia	157	
1932 Philadelphia	169		1930 Philadelphia	165	
1933 Philadelphia	163		1932 Philadelphia	151	
1938 Boston	175				

H. Greenberg			J. DiMaggio		
1935 Detroit	170		1937 New York	167	
1937 Detroit	183		1948 New York	155	
1940 Detroit	150				

K. Williams			H Trosky		
1922 St. Louis	155		1936 Texas	157	

V. Stephens			T. Williams		
1949 Boston	159		1949 Boston	159	

J. Gonzalez		A. Belle	
1998 Texas	157	1998 Cleveland	152
M. Ramirez		M. Tejada	
1999 Cleveland	165	2004 Baltimore	150
A. Rodriguez			
2007 New York	156		

National League

H. Wilson		S. Sosa	
1929 Chicago 159		1998 Chicago 158	
1930 Chicago 191		2001 Chicago 160	
R. Hornsby		M. Ott	
1922 St. Louis	152	1929 New York	151
C. Klein		J. Medwick	
1930 Philadelphia	170	1937 St. Louis	154
T. Davis		A. Galarraga	
1962 Los Angeles	153	1996 Colorado	150

Facts on the 150 RBI Mark

Only five men have done it in consecutive years.

Lou Gehrig: 1930 thru 1932
                    1936 thru 1937
Babe Ruth: 1929 thru 1931
Al Simmons: 1929 thru 1930
Hack Wilson: 1929 thru 1930
Jimmy Foxx: 1932 thru 1933

Lou Gehrig and Babe Ruth are the only men to do it in three consecutive years.

Lou Gehrig is the only man to have consecutive years of fifteen or more RBI's twice.

Jimmy Foxx is the only man to have 159 RBI seasons with two different teams.
Philadelphia 1930, 1932 and 1933
Boston 1938

Batters That Have One Hundred Fifty Bases on Balls in a Season.

In 1996, Barry Bonds became the first National Leaguer to receive one hundred fifty or more bases on balls. Before that, only Babe Ruth and Ted Williams got one hundred fifty or more free passes in a season. In 1998, Mark McGwire who set the National record with one hundred sixty-two, joined Bonds. That was short lived as Bonds set the Major League record in 2001. That was quickly shredded as Bonds received an amazing total of one hundred ninety-eight in 2002.

American League

1932	B. Ruth	New York	170
1946	T. Williams	Boston	156
1947	T. Williams	Boston	162
1949	T. Williams	Boston	162

National League

1996	B. Bonds	San Francisco	151
1998	M. McGwire	San Francisco	162
2001	B. Bonds	San Francisco	177
2002	B. Bonds	San Francisco	198

Men with Fifty or More Home Runs and 150 or More RBI's in the Same Season

When Barry Bonds set the all-time season home record at seventy-three, Sammy Sosa came in second with sixty-four. Along with those homers were one hundred sixty RBI's. Sosa's year seemed just as significant and historical as Bonds' achievement. Taking Sammy's stats in those two areas, we can see some milestones tied and set. He became only the third man to get fifty plus homers and one hundred fifty plus RBI's twice. If we expanded his feat, we can show credence that he is the only man to hit sixty or more homers and drive in one hundred fifty or more runs in a two seasons. This puts him in a class by himself.

American League

			HR's	RBI's
B. Ruth	New York	1921	59	171
	New York	1927	60	164
J. Foxx	Philadelphia	1932	58	169
	Boston	1938	50	175

National League

			HR's	RBI's
S. Sosa	Chicago	1998	66	158
	Chicago	2001	64	160
H. Wilson	Chicago	1930	56	191

Men Who Led Both Leagues in Home Runs

Even with Inter-League Trading and free agency, this is a sparse list of four names. Eventually there will be additions. Notice one thing - that it took over eight decades before a third name was added.

B. Freeman	Washington	National League	1899	25
	Boston	American League	1903	13
S. Crawford	Cincinnati	National League	1901	16
	Detroit	American League	1908	7
F. McGriff	Toronto	American League	1989	36
	San Diego	National League	1992	35

M. McGwire	Oakland	American League	1987	49
	Oakland	American League	1996	52
	St. Louis	National League	1998	70
	St. Louis	National League	1999	66

Batters with Two Hundred Hits in a Season but No .300 Batting Average.

Jo Jo Moore of the New York Giants set a precedent for two hundred hits in a season. He gathered two hundred one hits and failed to reach a batting average of .300. Four more followed his example in the National League. In 1979, the American League saw their first batter get two hundred hits but failed to hit the magic .300 average.

National League			Hits	BA
1935	J. Moore	New York	201	.295
1962	M. Wills	Los Angles	208	.299
1967	L. Brock	St. Louis	206	.299
1970	M. Alou	Pittsburgh	201	.297
1973	R. Garr	Atlanta	200	.299

American League			Hits	BA
1979	B. Bell	Texas	200	.299
1985	B. Buckner	Boston	201	.299

Teams with Five or More One Hundred Run Scores

The first time a team had five or more men score one hundred or more runs in a season was the Philadelphia A's of 1929. That is one reason why they cakewalked to the pennant. Two years later, the New York Yankees topped the A's when they sent six century scorers across the plate. The problem was the Yankees could score but finished second thirteen and a half games behind the A's. In fact, that 1931 team was the third Major League team to score over 1000 runs. Seven other teams had five or more one hundred run scores. The Brooklyn Dodgers of 1953 became the only

National League team to have not just five, but six one hundred run scores. They, along with the 1931 Yankees, have achieved that milestone.

Teams with Five or More 100 Run Scores

American League

<u>1931   New York</u>
L. Gehrig	163
B. Ruth	149
E. Coombs	120
B. Chapman	120
J. Sewell	102
L. Lary	100

<u>1929   Philadelphia</u>
J. Foxx	123
M. Hass	115
A. Simmons	114
M. Cochrane	113
M. Bishop	102

<u>1934   Detroit</u>
C. Gehringer	134
H. Greenberg	118
B. Rogell	114
G. Goslin	106
P. Fox	101

<u>1938   New York</u>
R. Rolfe	132
J. DiMaggio	129
L. Gehrig	115
F. Crosetti	113
T. Henrich	109

<u>1941   New York</u>
J. DiMaggio	122
R. Rolfe	106
T. Henrich	106
J. Gordon	104
C. Keller	102

<u>1950   Boston</u>
D. DiMaggio	131
V. Stephens	125
J. Pesky	112
B. Doerr	103
W. Dropo	101

<u>1997   Seattle</u>
K. Griffey Jr.	125
J. Cora	105
J. Buhner	104
E. Martinez	104
A. Rodriguez	100

<u>2000   Chicago</u>
R. Durham	121
F. Thomas	115
C. Lee	107
J. Valentin	107
M. Ordonez	102

National League

1953   Brooklyn
D. Snider   132
J. Gilliam   125
J. Robinson   109
P. Reese   108
R. Campanella 103
G. Hodges   101

Teams with Three or More Hitters with Two Hundred Hits in a Season

There are well over sixty teams that have had two or more two hundred hit men in the same season. If we just concentrate on the teams that have three or more, we see that number is pared down to only eleven. Two of those clubs had four men that gathered two hundred hits in a season. On oddity was in the National League. During the 1929 pennant race, the Philadelphia Phillies became the first team to have four two hundred hit men. The Phillies would finish fifth with a losing record. The reason for this was that the Phillies played feats in the friendly confine against a not-so-good Phillies pitching staff.

Teams with Three or More Hitters with Two Hundred Hits in a Season
American League

1920   St. Louis
G. Sisler   257
B. Jacobson   216
J. Tobin   202

1921   St. Louis
J. Tobin   236
G. Sisler   216
B. Jacobson   211

1929   Detroit
D. Alexander 215
C. Gehringer 215
R. Johnson   201

1937   Detroit
G. Walker   213
C. Gehringer 209
P. Fox   208
H. Greenberg 200

1982   Milwaukee
R. Yount   210
C. Cooper   208
P. Molitor   201

1991   Texas
R. Sierra   203
R. Palmeiro   203
J. Franco   201

National League

1929   Philadelphia
L. O'Doul   254
C. Klein   219
F. Thompson 202
P. Whitney   200

1930   Chicago
K. Cuyler   228
W. English   214
H. Wilson   208

1930   Philadelphia
C. Klein   250
P. Whitney   207
L. O'Doul   202

1935   New York
W. Terry   203
H. Leiber   203
J. Moore   201

1963   St. Louis
D. Groat   201
B. White   200
C. Flood   200

Men with Two Hundred Hits a Season in both Leagues

One of the greatest hitters in the game had two hundred hits a season six times. This all took place during the 1920's. Five of those years, Sisler had two hundred hits with the St. Louis Browns. In 1928, White with the Washington Senators was traded to the National League's Boston Braves. In 1929, George delivers two hundred five hits for the cellar-dwelling Braves. The next time a man would get two hundred hits a season in both leagues would be in the 1980's. Three times that has taken place.

Men with Two Hundred Hits a season in both Leagues

G. Sisler	St. Louis	American League	1920	257
	St. Louis	American League	1921	216
	St. Louis	American League	1922	246
	St. Louis	American League	1925	224
	St. Louis	American League	1927	2
	Boston	National League	1929	205
A. Oliver	Texas	American League	1980	209
	Montreal	National League	1982	204
B. Buckner	Chicago	National League	1982	201
	Boston	American League	1985	201
S. Sax	Los Angeles	National League	1986	210
	New York	American League	1989	205

Men with Two Hundred Hits a Season Two or More Teams

Nap LaJoie was the first to do this in the American League when he got two hundred twenty-nine with Philadelphia and made two hundred eleven with Cleveland in 1904. In the National League, Milt Stock was the first senior circuit player to do the feat. Rogers Hornsby in 1929 became the first man to get two hundred plus hits for three different teams. He was the only one to claim that distinction until Paul Molitor amassed two hundred twenty-five hits for the Minnesota Twins.

American League

P. Molitor			N. LaJoie		
Milwaukee	1982	201	Philadelphia	1901	229
Minnesota	1991	216	Cleveland	1904	211
Toronto	1993	211	Cleveland	1906	214
Minnesota	1996	225	Cleveland	1910	227

J. Jackson			T. Speaker		
Cleveland	1911	233	Boston	1912	222
Chicago	1916	202	Cleveland	1916	211
Cleveland	1920	214			

A. Simmons			H. Manush		
Philadelphia	1925	253	St. Louis	1928	241
Philadelphia	1929	212	Washington	1932	214
Philadelphia	1930	211			
Philadelphia	1931	200			
Philadelphia	1932	216			
Chicago	1933	200			

J. Vosmik			D. Cramer		
Cleveland	1935	216	Philadelphia	1934	202
Boston	1938	201	Philadelphia	1935	214
			Boston	1940	200

R. Radcliff		
Chicago	1936	207
St. Louis	1940	200

National League

R. Hornsby

St. Louis	1920	218
St. Louis	1921	235
St. Louis	1922	250
St. Louis	1924	227
St. Louis	1925	203
New York	1927	205
Chicago	1929	229

P. Rose

Cincinnati	1965	209
Cincinnati	1966	205
Cincinnati	1968	210
Cincinnati	1969	218
Cincinnati	1970	205
Cincinnati	1973	230
Cincinnati	1975	210
Cincinnati	1976	215
Cincinnati	1977	204
Philadelphia	1979	208

M. Stock

| St. Louis | 1920 | 204 |
| Brooklyn | 1925 | 202 |

L. O'Doul

Philadelphia	1929	254
Philadelphia	1930	202
Brooklyn	1932	219

W. Keeler

Baltimore	1894	219
Baltimore	1895	213
Baltimore	1896	210
Baltimore	1897	239
Baltimore	1898	216
Baltimore	1899	216
Brooklyn	1900	204
Brooklyn	1901	202

Shortstop Batting Leaders

Noted for their fielding expertise instead of their hitting exploits, shortstops have on occasion led the leagues in several hitting categories. In batting average, the early part of the twentieth century saw Honus Wagner dominate this category with eight titles in the National League. Twenty-four years later the next shortstop copped the title. Twenty-five years after that, the last Senior Circuit shortstop that towed in the title was Dick Groat. Oddly, of the ten batting titles won by the three men, all were Pirates.

In the American League, only two men won titles up to 1996. With the new breed of offensive shortstops, two more added three titles. In the RBI leadership A-Rod became only fifth to add his name as a short stop. He joined Vern Stephens as the only junior circuit member.

With A-Rod spearheading the new breed of slugging shortstops, he has added his name with Robin Yount as the only American Leaguer to lead in slugging percentage and total bases. In the hit leadership, the new breed has led in total hits from 1997 through 1999. In the National League, Rich Aurilia topped the list in 2001, becoming the first since 1918, to be hit leader.

Batting Average
American League

1936	L. Appling	Chicago	.388
1943	L. Appling	Chicago	.328
1944	L. Boudreau	Seattle	.327
1996	A. Rodriguez	Seattle	.358
1999	N.Garciaparra	Boston	.379
2000	N.Garciaparra	Boston	.372

National League

1900	H. Wagner	Pittsburgh	.381
1903	H. Wagner	Pittsburgh	.355
1904	H. Wagner	Pittsburgh	.349
1906	H. Wagner	Pittsburgh	.339

1907	H. Wagner	Pittsburgh	.350
1908	H. Wagner	Pittsburgh	.354
1909	H. Wagner	Pittsburgh	.339
1911	H. Wagner	Pittsburgh	.334
1935	A. Vaughan	Pittsburgh	.385
1960	D. Groat	Pittsburgh	.325
2009	H. Ramirez	Florida	.342
2011	J. Reyes	New York	.337

Home Run

American League

1945	V. Stephens	St. Louis	24
2001	A. Rodriguez	Texas	52
2002	A. Rodriguez	Texas	57
2003	A. Rodriguez	Texas	47

National League

1958	E. Banks	Chicago	47
1960	E. Banks	Chicago	41

RBI's

American League

1944	V. Stephens	St. Louis	109
1949	V. Stephens	St. Louis	159
1950	V. Stephens	St. Louis	144
2001	A. Rodriguez	Texas	142
2004	M. Tejada	Baltimore	150

National League

1904	B. Dahlen	New York	80
1907	H. Wagner	Pittsburgh	91
1908	H. Wagner	Pittsburgh	106
1909	H. Wagner	Pittsburgh	102

| 1958 | E. Banks | Chicago | 129 |
| 1959 | E. Banks | Chicago | 143 |

Slugging Percentage

American League

| 1982 | R. Yount | Milwaukee | .578 |
| 2003 | A. Rodriguez | Texas | .600 |

National League

1900	H. Wagner	Pittsburgh	.572
1902	H. Wagner	Pittsburgh	.467
1904	H. Wagner	Pittsburgh	.520
1907	H. Wagner	Pittsburgh	.513
1908	H. Wagner	Pittsburgh	.542
1909	H. Wagner	Pittsburgh	.489
1958	E. Banks	Chicago	.614

Total Bases

American League

1982	R. Yount	Milwaukee	367
1996	A. Rodriguez	Seattle	379
2001	A. Rodriguez	Seattle	393
2002	A. Rodriguez	Texas	389

National League

1904	H. Wagner	Pittsburgh	255
1906	H. Wagner	Pittsburgh	237
1907	H. Wagner	Pittsburgh	264
1908	H. Wagner	Pittsburgh	308
1909	H. Wagner	Pittsburgh	242
1918	C. Hollocher	Chicago	202
1958	E. Banks	Chicago	379

Hits

<u>American League</u>

1941	C. Travis	Washington	218
1942	J. Pesky	Boston	205
1946	J. Pesky	Boston	208
1947	J. Pesky	Boston	209
1953	H. Kuenn	Detroit	209
1954	H. Kuenn	Detroit	201
1956	H. Kuenn	Detroit	196
1968	B. Campaneris	Oakland	177
1997	N. Garciaparra	Boston	209
1998	A. Rodriguez	Seattle	213
1999	D. Jeter	New York	219

<u>National League</u>

1908	H. Wagner	Pittsburgh	201
1910	H. Wagner	Pittsburgh	178
1910	H. Wagner	Pittsburgh	178
1918	C. Hollocher	Chicago	161
2001	R. Aurilia	San Francisco	206

<u>Catchers Leading in Batting Categories</u>

It is not too often that catchers will lead the league in a major batting stat. Only three times were they able to win a batting title. Only one man was a home run leader, and he did it twice. Four were league leaders in RBI's, and once a catcher lead the league in total bases. Why is this so? Most catchers do not play every team's games behind the plate due to the rigors of the position.

Batting Average

National League

1926	E. Hargrave	Cincinnati	.353
1938	E. Lombardi	Cincinnati	.342
1942	E. Lombardi	Boston	.330
2012	B. Posey	San Francisco	.336

American League

2006	J. Mauer	Minnesota	.347
2008	J. Mauer	Minnesota	.328
2009	J. Mauer	Minnesota	.365

Home Runs

American League	National League		
Never Accomplished	1970	J. Bench	45
	1974	J. Bench	40

Runs Batted In

National League

1953	R. Campanella	Brooklyn	141
1970	J. Bench	Cincinnati	148
1972	J. Bench	Cincinnati	125
1974	J. Bench	Cincinnati	129
1984	G. Carter	Montreal	106
1992	D. Daulton	Philadelphia	109

American League
Never Accomplished

Total Bases

American League	National League		
Never Accomplished	1974	J. Bench	Cincinnati	315

Batters leading league in RBI's with Two Different Teams

Considering the advent of free agency and inter-league trading, this is a very short list consisting of only seven names. In the case for Heinie Zimmerman his league, researchers dispute leading total in 1912. This is the year some credit him with the batting Triple Crown. Other researches give the RBI title to Honus Wagner. Until there is proof that is more substantial, we will just leave it as is.

American League

N. LaJoie	1902	Philadelphia	125
	1904	Cleveland	102
B. Ruth	1919	Boston 112	
	1920	New York	137
	1921	New York	171
	1923	New York	131
	1926	New York	145
	1928	New York	142
J. Foxx	1932	Philadelphia	169
	1933	Philadelphia	163
	1938	Boston	175
V. Stephens	1944	St. Louis	109
	1949	Boston	159
	1950	Boston	144

National League

H. Zimmerman	1912	Chicago	98
	1917	New York	100
J. Mize	1940	St. Louis	137
	1942	New York	110
	1947	New York	138

Switch Hitting Batting Leaders

Only eleven times in the history of baseball has switch-hitting have won batting (seven in the National League, four in the American League). Scanning the list of champions, you will be surprised that Mickey Mantle would be the first switch-hitter to win a batting title, which he did in 1956.

With home run leaders there has only been seven in both leagues combined. Mantle has laid claim to four of them himself.

In the RBI Category, only four names appear on the list, with Mantle winning his only title in his Triple Crown year of 1956. Surprisingly, the only National Leaguer to cop the RBI title is none other than Howard Johnson in 1991, with the New York Mets.

As far as the slugging leaders go, only six times did a switch-hitter win the crown. Mantle owns four of these.

Total base leaders shows that six times switch-hitters topped the charts. Six different men won, with Frankie Frisch of the New York Giants back in 1923 being the first.

With the hit leaders, the National League had thirteen years when a switch-hitter led the league. Pete Rose and Terry Pendleton are the only ones with multiple titles. Willie Wilson is the only American Leaguer to pace the league.

Batting Average

American League

M. Mantle	New York	1956	.353
W. Wilson	KC	1982	.332
B. Williams	New York	1998	.339
B. Mueller	Boston	2003	.326

National League

| P. Rose | 1968 | Cincinnati | .335 |
| P. Rose | 1969 | Cincinnati | .348 |

P. Rose	1973	Cincinnati	.338
W. McGee	1985	St. Louis	.353
W. McGee	1990	St. Louis	.335
T. Raines	1986	Montana	.334
T. Pendleton	1991	Atlanta	.319
C. Jones	2008	Atlanta	.364
J. Reyes	2011	New York	.337

Home Runs

American League

M. Mantle	New York	1955	37
M. Mantle	New York	1956	52
M. Mantle	New York	1958	42
M. Mantle	New York	1960	40
E. Murray	Baltimore	1981	22
M. Teixeira	New York	2009	39

National League

R. Collins	St. Louis	1934	35
H. Johnson	New York	1991	38

RBI's

American League

M. Mantle	New York	1956	130
E. Murray	Baltimore	1981	78
R. Sierra	Texas	1989	119
M. Teixeira	New York	2009	122

National League

H. Johnson	New York	1991	117

Switch Hitters Leading in Batting Categories

Hits

American League

1980	W. Wilson	KC	230

National League

1923	F. Frisch	New York	223
1957	R. Schoendienst	New York/ Milwaukee	200
1965	P. Rose	Cincinnati	209
1968	P. Rose	Cincinnati	210
1970	P. Rose	Cincinnati	205
1972	P. Rose	Cincinnati	198
1973	P. Rose	Cincinnati	230
1976	P. Rose	Cincinnati	215
1979	G. Templeton	St. Louis	211
1981	P. Rose	Philadelphia	140
1985	W. McGee	St. Louis	216
1991	T. Pendleton	Atlanta	187
1992	T. Pendleton	Atlanta	199
2008	J. Reyes	New York	204

Slugging

American League

1955	M. Mantle	New York	.611
1956	M. Mantle	New York	.705
1961	M. Mantle	New York	.687
1962	M. Mantle	New York	.605
1989	R. Sierra	Texas	.543

National League

1934	R. Collins	St. Louis	.615

Total Bases

American League

M. Mantle	New York	1956	376
R. Smith	Boston	1971	302
R. Sierra	Texas	1989	344

National League

F. Frisch	New York	1923	311
R. Collins	St. Louis	1934	369
T. Pendleton	Atlanta	1991	303

Batters with Combined Two Hundred Hits with Two Teams in the Same Season

In 1999, Randy Velarde collected two hundred hits for two teams in the American League. It was the first time it happened in the Junior Circuit. He joined three National Leaguers who previously did it.

American League

R. Velarde	1999	Colorado/Oakland	200

National League

Red Schoendienst	1957	New York/Milwaukee	200
Lou Brock	1964	Chicago/St. Louis	200
Willie Montanez	1976	San Francisco/Atlanta	206

Power Hitting Second Basemen

There have been a few occasions that the position not known for power hitting has had a key stone position. Forty homer man and once a one hundred fifty RBI man, Rogers Hornsby is the only one to be listed with forty plus homers and one hundred fifty plus RBI.

Forty Home Run Season

American League
Never Accomplished

National League
1922	R. Hornsby	St. Louis	42
1973	D. Johnson	Atlanta	42
1990	R. Sandberg	Chicago	42

150 RBI Season

American League
Never Accomplished

National League
1922	R. Hornsby	St. Louis	152

Power Hitting Shortstops

Another position not known for power hitting, shortstops could only claim two men who topped the forty-homer mark. With the emergence of the power hitting shortstops during the 1990's, forty homers not only surpassed, but the fifty mark as well. This can be attributed to Alex Rodriguez.

As of now, only Vern Stephens has reached one hundred fifty plus RBI's by a shortstop in a season.

Forty Home Run Seasons

American League
1969	R. Petrocelli	Boston	40
1998	A. Rodriguez	Seattle	42
1999	A. Rodriguez	Seattle	42
2000	A. Rodriguez	Seattle	41
2002	A. Rodriguez	Texas	57
2003	A. Rodriguez	Texas	47

National League

1955	E. Banks	Chicago	44
1958	E. Banks	Chicago	47
1959	E. Banks	Chicago	45
1960	E. Banks	Chicago	41
2001	A. Rodriguez	Texas	52

150 RBI Season

American League
1949	V. Stephens	Boston	159

National League
Never Accomplished

Catchers with Forty Plus Home Run Seasons

This is a feat that has been accomplished seven times. Due to the rigorous powering backstops taken during a game, it can be realized how difficult it is for a catcher to reach forty plus homers.

American League
Never Accomplished

National League
1953	R. Campanella	Brooklyn	40
1970	J. Bench	Cincinnati	45
1974	J. Bench	Cincinnati	40
1996	T. Hundley	New York	41
1997	M. Piazza	Los Angeles	40
1999	M. Piazza	New York	40
2003	J. Lopez	Atlanta	42

Pitchers with Thirty Win Seasons since 1900

With the scarcity of twenty game winners today it is almost impossible to expect anyone to match Denny McLain's thirty-one wins in 1968. Listed are those thirty game winners of modern times with the only two forty game victors of the twentieth century.

Pitchers with Forty or More Victories in a Season

American League

Name	Year	Opponent	Score	Hits	Losing Pitcher	Total Victories
Jack Chesbro	1904	Boston	3-2	4	Gibson	41
Jack Chesbro	1904	St. Louis	6-0	7	Glade	41
Ed Walsh	1908	Detroit	6-1	4	Mullins	40

National League
No Forty game wins

Pitchers with Thirty or More Victories in a Season
with the Thirtieth Victory Shown
American League

Name	Year	Opponent	Score	Hits	Losing Pitcher	Total Victories
C. Young	1901	Boston	5-2		Callahan	33
C. Young	1902	St. Louis	6-5	10	Donahue	32
J. Chesbro	1904	Detroit	2-1	5	Kitson	41
E. Walsh	1908	Boston	2-1	6	Arellanes	40
J. Coombs	1910	Chicago	3-1	2	Walsh	31
J. Wood	1912	Washington	1-0	6	Johnson	34
W. Johnson	1912	Detroit	6-3	6	Troy	33
W. Johnson	1913	New York	1-0	3	Ford	36
J. Bagby	1920	St. Louis	9-5	10	Bayne	31
R. Grove	1931	Chicago	3-1	5	Faber	31
D. McLain	1963	Oakland	5-4	6	Segui	31

Pitchers with Thirty or more Victories in a Season
with Thirtieth Victory Shown

National League

Name	Year	Opponent	Score	Hits	LP	Total Victories
McGinnity	1903	Chicago	6-2	8	Taylor	31
Mathewson	1903	Chicago	8-3	11	Currie	30
McGinnity	1904	Boston	8-7	14	Fisher	35
Mathewson	1904	Philadelphia	4-1	6	Sparks	33
Mathewson	1905	Pittsburgh	10-4	6	Phillippe	31
Mathewson	1908	Philadelphia	5-1	6	McQuillan	37
Alexander	1915	Chicago	5-1	5	Adams	31
Alexander	1916	Cincinnati	7-3	12	Schultz	33
Alexander	1917	New York	8-2	7	Benton	30
D. Dean	1934	Cincinnati	9-0	7	Johnson	30

Pitchers with Ten or More Shutouts in a Season

Cy Young 1904: The first in modern times to accomplish the feat. His first shutout was a perfect game against the Philadelphia A's. His shutout of the New York Highlanders on 10/8 kept Boston in first place. He has shutout every opponent at least once.

Ed Walsh 1906: Had only two blankings going into August. Walsh pitched six during that month, a Major League record. Two of those were one-hitters.

Ed Walsh 1908: Set a modern record of eleven in a season. Mathewson tied this in the same year in the National League. He Tied his major league of six in a month, during the furious 1908 pennant race in September. An oddity in that Walsh pitched all his shutouts at home.

Jack Coombs 1910: Set the modern major league record for seasonal shutouts at thirteen, to be broken in 1916, by Alexander. Coombs did not pitch his first until late June. Two of his totals were 0-0 ties. The one on 8/4 went sixteen innings against Walsh of the White Sox. He tossed five in the month of July.

Joe Wood 1912: Of his ten, one is a classic pitching duel. During the season, Walter Johnson set an American League record for consecutive wins at sixteen. During the streak, Wood was matching Johnson with his own streak. Wood had thirteen in a row when the Senators came to Boston. Washington moved Johnson's schedule start up a game with the chance stopping Wood. In a storybook setting, Wood defeated Johnson one to zero for his fourteenth straight. Wood went on to win two more giving sixteen and a share of the American League record.

Walter Johnson 1913: Topped Wood's total of the previous year by one. Of his eleven, five were by the score of one to zero. His best effort was a fifteen inning one to zero wins over World Series winner Boston.

Bob Feller 1946: pitched second career no hitter against the Yank's on 4/30. It was 0-0 until the top of the ninth. His catcher Frank Hayes hit a home run giving him the victory. A short while later Hayes was traded to the White Sox. On 8/8, Feller pitched a one hitter against the Sox and the culprit who spoiled his potential no-hitter was none other than Frank Hayes. Another tidbit of information in Fellers no-hitter on 4/30 was that the centerfielder was Bob Lemon. Two years later Lemon would duplicate Feller's year with ten shutouts and a no-hitter.

Bob Lemon 1948: He duplicated Feller's ten shutouts and one no-hitter of 1946. Seven of Lemon's ten gems were done on the road.

Dean Chance 1964: Did his feat for an expansion team in its fourth year of existence. His eleven blanks were the most since Johnson in 1913; he threw three of his eleven against the pennant winning Yankees.

Jim Palmer 1975: Of his ten shutouts, two were against the future American League winner Boston. Both were by the score of three to zero. His shutout of Kansas City on 6/8 was a one-hitter.

Christie Mathewson 1908: Tied with Walsh for new major league record, which would be broken two years later by Jack Coombs. His shutout of Boston on 4/27 was a one-hitter he shutout every opponent that year.

Grover Cleveland Alexander 1915: Set National League record for shutouts. Four of his shutouts were one-hitters. He shutout every opponent at least once. On 6/26, he blanked Brooklyn and Coombs four to zero. Coombs at the time held the Major League record. He defeated New York on 9/2 besting the legendary Mathewson in a rare match up.

Grover Cleveland Alexander1916: Set all time Major League record at sixteen. His fourteenth set the modern record on 9/1 versus Brooklyn. He ironically defeated Coombs who held the Major League record. He again shut out every opponent at least once. Nine of his sixteen whitewashes were done at home, which was the "Band Box" Baker's Bowl. It amazes historians how he was able to do it in such a miniscule field.

Carl Hubbell 1933: The first left-hander to fashion ten shutouts during a season. Half of his shutouts were by the score of one to zero. On 7/2, he pitched a 1-0 game that went eighteen innings against St. Louis. Cardinal starter Tex Carleton quit after the sixteenth. Reliever Jesse Haines yielded the winning run in the bottom of the eighteenth. The second game was also a one to zero contest won by the Giants. Hubbell's year won him the league most valuable player.

Mort Cooper 1942: Three of his ten shutouts came against rival Brooklyn. The Cardinals came from ten and a half games back in August to nose out Brooklyn by two games. Cooper threw three shutouts against Brooklyn that were the difference in the final standings. His 9/11 gem against the Dodgers made him the league's first twenty game winner. On 9/24, he clinched a tie for the pennant with his tenth shutout. Like Hubbell, he was voted the league's most valuable player.

Sandy Koufax 1963: He became the second lefty to pitch ten or more shutouts in a season. His shutout of the Cardinals in 9/17 gave him the record for shutouts by a southpaw at eleven. On 5/11, he pitched his second no-hitter against the hated Giants. His outstanding year earned him both most valuable player and the CY Young award.

Juan Marichal 1965: Became the third giant pitcher to spin ten or more shutouts in a season, joining Mathewson and Hubbell. Four of his ten came against the lowly Mets, against whom he always had fantastic success.

Bob Gibson 1968: Pitched the most seasonal shutouts at thirteen since Alexander's sixteen in 1916. Gibson pitched his first shutout two months after the season began. In the month of June, he became one of three pitchers who threw five consecutive whitewashes. This earned him like Koufax, both most valuable player and the CY Young award.

John Tudor 1985: The Cardinals, like the Giants, now had three pitchers with ten or more shutouts in a season. The curious thing about Tudor's year was he started the year at one to seven while finishing at twenty-one to eight. He won twenty of his last twenty-one decisions with half of the victories being shutouts. He started his run of stellar pitching when he defeated the Mets one to zero on 6/8 at Shea Stadium. In his game on 8/8, he one-hit the Cubs, with Leon Durham getting the hit. On 9/11, with the Eastern Division lead hanging in the balance, he again topped the Mets one to zero at Shea. Those wins against the Amazing Mets were the difference in St. Louis winning the division. Due to Dwight Gooden's career season Tudor was deprived of the CY Young award.

Dave Davenport 1915: Pitching in the short-lived Federal League for the St. Louis Terriers, Davenport tossed ten shutouts. He was one of three twenty game winners on that team which finished second, .001 behind the pennant winner Chicago Whales. That made the race the closest in baseball history. Dave's blank included a zero to zero with Pittsburgh. On 7/31, Davenport almost duplicated the doubleheader shutout feat of the Cubs Ed Ruelbach in 1908. In the first game he defeated Buffalo one to zero on four hits. Left fielder Ward Miller stole home to give Davenport the win in game two; he gave up a double by Hal Chase. This was the only hit for Buffalo. Chase came home on a sacrifice fly by Solly Hoffman. Davenport's two games totals was one run and five hits in eighteen innings of pitching. On 9/7, Davenport threw a no-hitter against eventual pennant winner Chicago.

Cy Young Boston 1904 American League Ten Shutouts

	Date	Team	Score	Hits	Loser
H	5/1	Philadelphia	3-0	0	Waddell
H	5/11	Detroit	1-0	5	Killian
A	6/6	Detroit	3-0	3	Killian
A	7/6	Washington	3-0	7	Jacobson
A	8/1	Cleveland	8-0	5	Bernhard
H	8/22	St. Louis	8-0	7	Glade
H	8/30	Detroit	13-0	6	Kitson
A	10/2	St. Louis	2-0	3	Pelty

	Date	Team	Score	Hits	Loser
A	10/5	Chicago	3-0	6	Altrock
H	10/8	New York	1-0	7	Powell

E. Walsh Chicago American League 1906 Ten Shutouts

	Date	Team	Score	Hits	Loser
H	5/6	Cleveland	6-0	1	Joss
H	6/14	Washington	2-0	5	Patten
H	8/3	Boston	4-0	1	Harris
H	8/7	Philadelphia	4-0	3	Waddell
H	8/12	New York	3-0	9	Orth
A	8/15	Boston 6-0	4		Tannehill
A	8/18	New York	10-0	5	Chesbro
A	8/27	Philadelphia	1-0	1	Coombs
H	9/14	St. Louis	3-0	3	Jacobson
H	9/26	Boston	2-0	6	Oberlin

E. Walsh Chicago American League 1908 Eleven Shutouts

	Date	Team	Score	Hits	Loser
H	4/18	St. Louis	3-0	3	Graham
H	5/3	Cleveland	3-0	6	Chech
H	5/31	Detroit	1-0	4	Willet
H	6/20	Boston	1-0	5	Young
H	8/7	Boston	7-0	4	Burchell
H	9/5	Cleveland	7-0	5	Joss
H	9/13	Cleveland	1-0	5	Berger
H	9/18	Washington	1-0	8	Johnson
H	9/21	Philadelphia	2-0	3	Schitzer
H	9/29	Boston	3-0	6	Cicotte
H	9/29	Boston	2-0	4	Steele

J. Coombs Philadelphia American League 1910 Thirteen Shutouts

	Date	Team	Score	Hits	Loser
A	6/22	New York	8-0	5	Warhop
H	7/1	New York	2-0	7	Ford
H	7/15	St. Louis	3-0	5	Pelty
H	7/20	Chicago	2-0	6	Young

H	7/23	Cleveland	2-0	3	Fanwell
H	7/29	Washington	4-0	6	Groom
A	8/4	Chicago	0-0	3	Walsh (16 Innings)
A	8/7	St. Louis	6-0	5	Lake
H	8/26	St. Louis	6-0	4	Pelty
A	9/9	Boston	2-0	6	Hunt
H	9/12	Washington	4-0	4	Reisling
A	9/16	Detroit	10-0	2	Willet
A	9/21	Cleveland	0-0	3	Fanwell

J. Wood Boston American League 1912 Ten Shutouts

	Date	Team	Score	Hits	Loser
H	5/20	Chicago	2-0	5	Walsh
A	6/26	Washington	3-0	3	Johnson
H	6/29	New York	6-0	1	Thompson (7 innings)
H	7/12	Detroit	1-0	5	Willet
A	8/2	St. Louis	9-0	3	Hamilton
H	8/14	St. Louis	8-0	4	Allison
H	8/28	Chicago	3-0	6	Taylor
A	9/2	New York	1-0	8	McConnell
H	9/6	Washington	1-0	6	Johnson
H	9/25	New York	6-0	2	Schulz

W. Johnson Washington American League 1913 Eleven Shutouts

	Date	Team	Score	Hits	Loser
A	4/19	New York	3-0	6	Keating
H	4/23	Boston	6-0	2	Collins
A	4/30	Philadelphia	2-0	4	Plank
A	5/10	Chicago	1-0	2	Benz
H	6/6	St. Louis	1-0	5	Leverenz
H	6/10	Detroit	3-0	2	Clauss
H	6/21	New York	6-0	2	Keating
H	6/27	Philadelphia	2-0	3	Brown
A	7/3	Boston	1-0	15	Collins (15 innings)
H	9/15	New York	1-0	3	Ford
H	9/29	Philadelphia	1-0	5	Wyckoff

B. Feller Cleveland American League 1946 Ten Shutouts

	Date	Team	Score	Hits	Loser
A	4/16	Chicago	1-0	3	Dietrich
A	4/30	New York	1-0	0	Bevens
H	5/17	Washington	3-0	5	Haefner
H	5/30	Chicago	3-0	8	Haynes
A	6/29	Chicago	2-0	4	Grove
H	7/3	St. Louis	6-0	10	Galehouse
H	7/24	Philadelphia	1-0	3	Savage
H	7/28	Washington	2-0	4	Newsom
A	8/8	Chicago	5-0	1	Grove
A	8/24	Philadelphia	5-0	8	Harris

Frank Hayes won the 4/30 game with a homer in the ninth. Hayes was later traded to Chicago when in the 8/8 game Frank Hayes was the one who got the hit that spoiled Fellers bid for his second no hitter of the year.

B. Lemon Cleveland American League 1948 Ten Shutouts

	Date	Team	Score	Hits	Loser
A	5/7	Washington	8-0	4	Haefner
H	5/25	Washington	4-0	4	Haefner
A	5/29	Chicago	4-0	4	Wright
H	6/20	Philadelphia	10-0	4	Marchildon
A	6/30	Detroit	2-0	0	Houtteman
H	7/11	St. Louis	5-0	3	Shore
A	8/15	Chicago	8-0	7	Haynes
A	8/25	Boston	9-0	4	Galehouse
A	8/29	Washington	6-0	7	Thompson
A	9/3	St. Louis	7-0	6	W. Kennedy

D. Chance Los Angeles American League 1964 Eleven Shutouts

	Date	Team	Score	Hits	Loser
A	5/24	New York	3-0	3	Bouton
H	6/2	Boston	1-0	2	Lamabe
H	6/23	Washington	2-0	4	Daniels

H	7/11	Chicago	1-0	4	Talbot
H	7/15	Detroit	1-0	5	Regan
A	7/19	Minnesota	4-0	4	Grant
A	8/14	Washington	7-0	2	Koch
A	8/18	Detroit	1-0	2	Aguirre
H	9/2	New York	4-0	4	Bouton
A	9/15	New York	7-0	2	Downing
H	9/25	Minnesota	1-0	8	Kaat

J. Palmer Baltimore American League 1975 Ten Shutouts

	Date	Team	Score	Hits	Loser
A	4/10	Detroit 10-0	3	Coleman	
A	4/22	Milwaukee	1-0	6	Broberg
H	5/16	California	1-0	9	Tanana
A	5/30	California	5-0	4	Figueroa
H	6/8	KC	1-0	1	Busby
H	6/21	Boston	3-0	5	Pole
A	8/5	Boston	3-0	2	Tiant
H	8/13	KC	3-0	2	Pattin
H	8/17	Texas	4-0	4	Perzanowski
H	9/28	New York	3-0	8	Kay

C. Mathewson NY National League 1908 Eleven Shutouts

	Date	Team	Score	Hits	Loser
A	4/18	Brooklyn	4-0	6	Pastorius
A	4/27	Boston	2-0	1	Young
A	5/29	Brooklyn	1-0	4	Rucker
A	6/3	Boston	3-0	3	Young
H	6/20	Chicago	4-0	3	Fraser
A	7/13	Pittsburgh	7-0	3	Leifeld
H	7/29	St. Louis	1-0	3	Sallee
A	8/17	St. Louis	3-0	4	Sallee
A	8/20	Cincinnati	2-0	8	Coakley
H	9/8	Brooklyn	1-0	5	Rucker
H	9/28	Pittsburgh	7-0	5	Maddox

G. Alexander National League 1915 Twelve Shutouts

	Date	Team	Score	Hits	Loser
A	4/14	Boston	3-0	6	Rudolph
H	5/25	Chicago	3-0	2	Humphries
A	6/5	St. Louis	3-0	1	Meadows
H	6/26	Brooklyn	4-0	1	Coombs
H	7/5	New York	2-0	1	Perritt
H	7/13	St. Louis	8-0	6	Griner
H	7/21	Chicago	1-0	2	Adams
H	7/24	Cincinnati	4-0	8	McKerney
H	8/25	Cincinnati	8-0	4	Schneider
A	9/2	New York	2-0	7	Mathewson
H	9/9	New York	3-0	3	Benton
A	9/29	Boston	5-0	1	Rudolph

G. Alexander National League 1916 Sixteen Shutouts

	Date	Team	Score	Hits	Loser
H	4/8	Boston	4-0	5	Rudolph
A	5/3	Boston	3-0	6	Barnes
A	5/13	Cincinnati	5-0	3	Dale
A	5/18	Pittsburgh	3-0	4	Kantlehner
H	5/26	Brooklyn	1-0	8	Smith
H	6/3	St. Louis	2-0	9	Meadows
A	7/7	Seattle	1-0	6	Meadows
A	7/15	Pittsburgh	4-0	4	Jacobs
A	7/20	Cincinnati	6-0	2	Toney
H	8/2	Chicago	1-0	7	Prendergast
H	8/9	Cincinnati	1-0	3	Schulz
H	8/14	New York	8-0	4	Benton
A	8/18	Cincinnati	3-0	7	Schneider
H	9/1	Brooklyn	3-0	8	Coombs
H	9/23	Cincinnati	4-0	8	Toney
H	10/2	Boston	2-0	3	Ragan

C. Hubbell NY National League 1933 Ten Shutouts

	Date	Team	Score	Hits	Loser
H	4/20	Boston	1-0	4	Frankhouse
H	4/24	Brooklyn	4-0	4	Shaute
H	5/7	Cincinnati	1-0	5	Smith
H	6/22	Cincinnati	4-0	5	Lucas
H	7/2	St. Louis	1-0	6	Haines (1st game 18 innings)
A	7/16	Cincinnati	1-0	8	Derringer
A	7/22	Pittsburgh	1-0	6	French
H	7/27	Brooklyn	2-0	4	Mungo
H	8/29	St. Louis	3-0	5	Hallahan
A	9/1	Boston	2-0	4	Frankhouse

9/1/33 first game Giants score two in top of the tenth.

M. Cooper St. Louis National League 1942 Ten Shutouts

	Date	Team	Score	Hits	Loser
H	4/21	Cincinnati	8-0	3	Walters
A	5/20	Brooklyn	1-0	2	Wyatt
H	6/2	New York	2-0	4	Carpenter
A	6/17	New York	3-0	5	Melton
A	6/21	Brooklyn	11-0	5	Head
A	6/25	Boston	4-0	2	Javery
H	8/13	Cincinnati	4-0	2	Derringer
A	9/11	Brooklyn	3-0	3	Wyatt
A	9/20	Chicago	1-0	4	Warneke
H	9/24	Cincinnati	6-0	2	Starr

S. Koufax Los Angeles National League 1963 Eleven Shutouts

	Date	Team	Score	Hits	Loser
H	4/19	Houston	2-0	2	Farrell
H	5/11	San Francisco	8-0	0	Marichal
H	5/19	New York	1-0	2	Craig
A	5/28	Milwaukee	7-0	7	Lemaster
H	6/13	Houston	3-0	3	Bruce
A	6/17	San Francisco	2-0	4	O'Dell

H	7/3	St. Louis	5-0	3	Gibson
H	7/7	Cincinnati	4-0	3	Purkey
A	7/12	New York	6-0	3	Jackson
A	8/3	Houston	2-0	3	Bruce
A	9/17	St. Louis	4-0	4	Simmons

J. Marichal San Francisco National League 1965 Ten Shutouts

	Date	Team	Score	Hits	Loser
A	4/17	New York	4-0	4	Parsons
H	4/25	New York	5-0	5	Jackson
A	6/5	Cincinnati	1-0	5	Maloney
A	6/10	New York	3-0	7	Kroll
H	6/28	Los Angeles	5-0	6	Drysdale
A	7/2	Chicago	4-0	5	Koonce
A	7/10	Philadelphia	7-0	2	Culp
H	7/17	Houston	7-0	5	Farrell
H	8/18	New York	5-0	3	L. Miller
H	9/9	Houston	4-0	4	Bruce

B. Gibson Seattle National League 1968 Thirteen Shutouts

	Date	Team	Score	Hits	Loser
A	6/6	Houston	4-0	3	Wilson
A	6/11	Atlanta	6-0	5	Kelley
H	6/15	Cincinnati	2-0	4	Nolan
H	6/20	Chicago	1-0	5	Jenkins
H	6/26	Pittsburgh	3-0	4	McBean
A	7/6	San Francisco	3-0	6	Marichal
H	7/21	New York	2-0	7	McAndrew
H	7/25	Philadelphia	5-0	5	Short
A	8/9	Atlanta	1-0	4	Niekro
A	8/19	Philadelphia	2-0	2	Fryman
A	8/28	Pittsburgh	8-0	4	Veale
A	9/2	Cincinnati	1-0	4	Abernathy
H	9/27	Houston	1-0	6	Dierker

J. Tudor Seattle National League 1985 Ten Shutouts

	Date	Team	Score	Hits	Loser
A	6/8	New York	1-0	3	Gorman
H	6/23	Chicago	7-0	2	Ruthven
A	7/2	Montana	4-0	3	Palmer
H	7/11	San Diego	6-0	5	Thurmond
A	7/24	San Francisco	4-0	6	Gott
H	8/8	Chicago	8-0	1	Sanderson
H	9/1	Houston	5-0	7	Niekro
H	9/6	Atlanta	8-0	7	Mahler
A	9/11	New York	1-0	3	Orosco
H	9/26	Philadelphia	5-0	4	Gross

D. Davenport Seattle Federal League 1915 Ten Shutouts

	Date	Team	Score	Hits	Loser
A	5/5	Brooklyn	3-0	6	Lafitte
H	5/31	Pittsburgh	0-0	5	Allen (9 innings darkness)
A	6/15	New York	1-0	2	Ruelbach
A	7/1	Buffalo	13-0	6	Bedient
H	7/31	Buffalo	1-0	4	Schulz
A	8/10	Buffalo	8-0	7	Bedient
H	9/5	Pittsburgh	6-0	5	Comstock
H	9/7	Chicago	3-0	0	Brennan
H	9/10	New York	3-0	2	Seaton
H	9/17	Brooklyn	2-0	2	Falkenberg

On 7/31, Davenport lost the second game to Buffalo one to zero, giving up one hit run scores in eighth.

Pitchers with Two Hundred Strikeouts in a Season
with Three Different Teams

When Roger Clemens struck out 213 batters for the Yankees in 2001, he joined Nolan Ryan and Kevin Brown as the only men to strikeout two hundred or more batters for three different teams. Clemens and Ryan are the only two to whiff two hundred or more men in three different decades.

Brown on the other hand is the only man to "K" two hundred batters in three consecutive years with three different teams.

N. Ryan
California	American League	1972	329
California	American League	1973	383
California	American League	1974	367
California	American League	1976	325
California	American League	1977	341
California	American League	1978	260
California	American League	1979	223
Houston	American League	1980	200
Houston	American League	1982	245
Houston	American League	1985	209
Houston	American League	1987	270
Houston	American League	1988	228
Texas	American League	1989	301
Texas	American League	1990	232
Texas	American League	1991	203

R. Clemens
Boston	American League	1986	238
Boston	American League	1987	236
Boston	American League	1988	291
Boston	American League	1989	230
Boston	American League	1990	209
Boston	American League	1991	241
Boston	American League	1992	208
Boston	American League	1996	297
Toronto	American League	1997	292
Toronto	American League	1998	271
New York	American League	2001	213

K. Brown
Florida	National League	1997	205
San Diego	National League	1988	257
Los Angeles	National League	1999	221
Los Angeles	National League	2000	216

Believe it or not, there are not that many. In the American League, there are seven, while in the National League five can claim that distinction. Randy Johnson has eight, which equally divide between both leagues. Nolan Ryan with his eleven titles has nine in the Junior Circuit, and two in the National League.

Leading League in Strikeouts Five or More Years.

American League

W. Johnson	1910	Washington	313
	1912	Washington	303
	1913	Washington	243
	1914	Washington	225
	1915	Washington	203
	1916	Washington	228
	1917	Washington	188
	1918	Washington	162
	1919	Washington	147
	1921	Washington	143
	1923	Washington	130
	1924	Washington	158
L. Grove	1925	Philadelphia	116
	1926	Philadelphia	194
	1927	Philadelphia	174
	1928	Philadelphia	183
	1929	Philadelphia	170
	1930	Philadelphia	209
	1931	Philadelphia	175
B. Feller	1938	Cleveland	240
	1939	Cleveland	246
	1940	Cleveland	261
	1941	Cleveland	260
	1946	Cleveland	348
	1947	Cleveland	196
	1948	Cleveland	164

R. Waddell	1902	Philadelphia	210
	1903	Philadelphia	301
	1904	Philadelphia	349
	1905	Philadelphia	286
	1906	Philadelphia	203
	1907	Philadelphia	226

S. McDowell	1965	Cleveland	325
	1966	Cleveland	225
	1968	Cleveland	283
	1969	Cleveland	279
	1970	Cleveland	304

R. Clemens	1988	Boston	291
	1991	Boston	241
	1996	Boston	257
	1997	Toronto	292

National League

C. Mathewson	1903	New York	267
	1904	New York	212
	1905	New York	206
	1907	New York	178
	1908	New York	259
	1910	New York	190
	1928	Brooklyn	200

D. Vance	1922	Brooklyn	134
	1923	Brooklyn	197
	1924	Brooklyn	262
	1925	Brooklyn	221
	1926	Brooklyn	140
	1926	Brooklyn	184

G. Alexander	1914	Philadelphia		214
	1915	Philadelphia		241
	1916	Philadelphia		167
	1917	Philadelphia		200
	1920	Philadelphia		173

T. Seaver	1970	New York		283
	1971	New York		289
	1973	New York		251
	1975	New York		243
	1976	New York		235

S. Carlton	1972	Philadelphia		310
	1974	Philadelphia		240
	1980	Philadelphia		286
	1982	Philadelphia		286
	1983	Philadelphia		275

Combined Leagues

N. Ryan	1972	California	American League	329
	1973	California	American League	383
	1974	California	American League	367
	1976	California	American League	327
	1977	California	American League	341
	1978	California	American League	260
	1979	California	American League	223
	1987	Houston	National League	270
	1988	Houston	National League	228
	1989	Texas	American League	201
	1990	Texas	American League	232

R. Johnson	1992	Seattle	American League	241
	1993	Seattle	American League	308
	1994	Seattle	American League	204
	1995	Seattle	American League	294
	1999	Arizona	National League	364

2000	Arizona	National League	347
2001	Arizona	National League	372
2002	Arizona	National League	334

*Note Johnson led Majors in strikeouts with 329. Pitched in both Leagues, Seattle 213, and Houston 113.

The Only Man to Pitch a No-Hitter and Lose

On April 23, 1964, Ken Johnson of the Houston Colt 45's pitched a no-hitter and lost. He became the only man in the history of the Major League to do that.

He was matched up with the Cincinnati Reds Joe Nuxhall. Nuxhall was famous for being the youngest to appear in a Major League game, at the ripe old age of fifteen years and ten months.

Johnson went into the ninth at zero to zero. In the top of the inning Johnson created his own downfall. Pete Rose laid down a bunt that should have been easily handled, but in his haste, Johnson threw wildly allowing Rose to go to second base.   Rose advanced to third on a ground out. The next batter grounded to sure hand Nellie Fox who booted the ball, which allowed Rose to score. Houston went quietly in the bottom of the ninth. Johnson, due to his own fault, gave himself the distinction of being the only man to pitch a no-hitter and lose. Conversely, Nuxhall became the only man to pitch against a no-hitter and win.

4/23/64 Ken Johnson, Houston vs. Cincinnati, zero to one at Houston

Pitchers Who Have Lead the League in Victories Four or More Times

This has occurred twelve times in the history of baseball. Warren Spahn has done it a record eight times in his career, which is the Major League record. In the American League the record is six shared by Walter Johnson and Bob Feller. One case of interest is Joe McGinnity, who is the only man to lead the league in victories with three different teams.

Also, in regard to Spahn, he is the only pitcher to lead his league in victories during three different decades.

102

American League

W. Johnson	Washington	American League	1913	36-7
	Washington	American League	1914	28-18
	Washington	American League	1915	27-13
	Washington	American League	1916	25-20
	Washington	American League	1918	23-13
	Washington	American League	1924	23-7
B. Feller	Cleveland	American League	1939	24-9
	Cleveland	American League	1940	27-11
	Cleveland	American League	1941	25-13
	Cleveland	American League	1946	26-9
	Cleveland	American League	1947	20-11
	Cleveland	American League	1951	22-8
L. Grove	Philadelphia	American League	1928	24-8
	Philadelphia	American League	1930	28-5
	Philadelphia	American League	1931	31-4
	Philadelphia	American League	1933	24-8
H. Newhouser	Detroit	American League	1944	29-9
	Detroit	American League	1945	25-9
	Detroit	American League	1946	26-9
	Detroit	American League	1948	21-12
R. Clemens	Boston	American League	1986	24-4
	Boston	American League	1987	20-9
	Toronto	American League	1997	21-7
	Toronto	American League	1998	20-6

National League

W. Spahn	Boston	National League	1949	21-14
	Boston	National League	1950	21-17
	Milwaukee	National League	1953	29-7
	Milwaukee	National League	1957	21-11
	Milwaukee	National League	1958	22-11
	Milwaukee	National League	1959	21-15
	Milwaukee	National League	1960	21-10
	Milwaukee	National League	1961	21-13

Grover Alexander

	Philadelphia	National League	1914	27-15
	Philadelphia	National League	1915	31-10
	Philadelphia	National League	1916	32-12
	Philadelphia	National League	1917	30-13
	Philadelphia	National League	1920	27-14
C. Mathewson	New York	National League	1905	31-9
	New York	National League	1907	24-12
	New York	National League	1907	24-12
J. McGinnity	Baltimore	National League	1899	28-7
	Brooklyn	National League	1900	29-9
	New York	National League	1903	31-20
	New York	National League	1904	35-8
	New York	National League	1906	27-12
S. Carlton	Philadelphia	National League	1972	27-10
	Philadelphia	National League	1977	23-10
	Philadelphia	National League	1977	23-10
	Philadelphia	National League	1980	24-9
	Philadelphia	National League	1982	23-11
R. Roberts	Philadelphia	National League	1952	28-7
	Philadelphia	National League	1953	23-16
	Philadelphia	National League	1954	23-15
	Philadelphia	National League	1955	23-14

Combined Leagues

C. Young	Cleveland	National League	1895	35-10
	Boston	American League	1901	33-10
	Boston	American League	1902	32-11
	Boston	American League	1903	28-9

Pitchers with Two Hundred Strikeout Seasons in Both Leagues
It would seem that with interleague trading and free agency that this list would be much longer. As of now, it has only occurred ten times. There is no doubt, in time more names will be added to the list. An interesting note is that as of now, Randy Johnson is the only one to have struck out three hundred batters in a season in both leagues.

J. Bunning	Detroit	American League	1959
	Detroit	American League	1960
	Philadelphia	National League	1964
	Philadelphia	National League	1965
	Philadelphia	National League	1966
	Philadelphia	National League	1967
D. Cone	New York	National League	1988
	New York	National League	1990
	New York	National League	1991
	New York	National League	1992
	New York	American League	1997
	New York	American League	1998
F. Jenkins	Chicago	National League	1967
	Chicago	National League	1968
	Chicago	National League	1969
	Chicago	National League	1970
	Chicago	National League	1971
	Texas	American League	1974
R. Johnson	Seattle	American League	1991
	Seattle	American League	1992
	Seattle	American League	1993
	Seattle	American League	1994
	Seattle	American League	1995
	Seattle	American League	1997
	Seattle	American League	1998
	Arizona	National League	1999
	Arizona	National League	2000
	Arizona	National League	2001
	Arizona	National League	2002

P. Martinez	Montreal	National League	1996
	Montreal	National League	1997
	Boston	American League	1998
	Boston	American League	1999
	Boston	American League	2000
	Boston	American League	2002
	Boson	American League	2003

A. Messersmith	California	American League	1969
	Los Angeles	National League	1974
	Los Angeles	National League	1975

H. Nomo	Los Angeles	National League	1995
	Los Angeles	National League	1996
	Los Angeles	National League	1997
	Boston	American League	2001

G. Perry	San Francisco	National League	1966
	San Francisco	National League	1967
	San Francisco	National League	1969
	San Francisco	National League	1970

N. Ryan	California	American League	1972
	California	American League	1973
	California	American League	1974
	California	American League	1976
	California	American League	1977
	California	American League	1978
	California	American League	1979
	Houston	National League	1980
	Houston	National League	1982
	Houston	National League	1985
	Houston	National League	1987
	Houston	National League	1988
	Texas	American League	1989
	Texas	American League	1990
	Texas	American League	1991

B. Singer	Los Angeles	National League	1968
	Los Angeles	National League	1969
	California	American League	1973

The Three Hundred Strikeout Pitchers

In 1903, Rube Waddell became the first man in modern history to strikeout three hundred or more batters in a season. In 1904, he set the modern day record of three hundred forty-nine that stood until Sandy Koufax obliterated it in 1965, with three hundred eighty-two "K". The uniqueness about the Rube's record was that in 1946, Bob Feller challenged its three hundred forty-eight. Everyone thought that Rapid Robert had a new record, but old times who didn't want to see cherished standards broken, scanned the archives. They came up with six more strikeouts for Wadell, which nullified any record that Feller might have created. Koufax in 1965 erased any doubts about the record.

N. Ryan
California	American League	1972	329
California	American League	1973	383
California	American League	1974	367
California	American League	1976	327
California	American League	1977	341
Texas	American League	1989	301

R. Johnson
Seattle	American League	1993	308
Seattle	American League		
Houston	National League	1998	329
Arizona	National League	1999	364
Arizona	National League	2001	372
Arizona	National League	2002	334

S. Koufax
Los Angeles	National League	1963	306
Los Angeles	National League	1965	382
Los Angeles	National League	1966	317

C. Schilling

Philadelphia	National League	1997	319
Philadelphia	National League	1998	300
Arizona	National League	2002	316

R. Waddell

Philadelphia	American League	1903	301
Philadelphia	American League	1904	349

W. Johnson

Washington	American League	1910	313
Washington	American League	1912	303

S. McDowell

Cleveland	American League	1965	325
Cleveland	American League	1970	304

J. Richard

Houston	National League	1978	303
Houston	National League	1979	313

P. Martinez

Montana	National League	1997	305
Boston	American League	1999	313

B. Feller

Cleveland	American League	1940	348

M. Lolich

Detroit	American League	1971	308

V. Blue

Oakland	American League	1971	301

S. Carlton

Philadelphia	National League	1972	310

M. Scott

Houston	National League	1986	306

Little Known Facts about Three Hundred-Strikeout Pitchers

1) Three pitchers with three hundred strikeouts failed to lead league.
Vida Blue - Oakland, American League 1971- 301
Pedro Martinez - Montana, National League 1997- 305
Curt Schilling - Arizona, National league 2002- 316

2) There are three years where both league leaders in strikeouts had three hundred or more.
1965, Koufax, National League and McDowell, American League
1972, Carlton, National League and Ryan, American League
1999, Johnson, National League and Martinez, American League

3) The only teammates to strikeout three hundred or more batters in the same year.
2002, R. Johnson (334) and C. Schilling (316) for Arizona.

Winning ERA Title with a Losing Record

It seems paradoxical that one can have a losing record and still come out on top in ERA. This has happened three times in the American League and five times in the Senior Circuit. On three occasions, the American League had three pitchers who had break-even records and won the ERA title.

American League

Name	Team	Year	W-L	Era
E. Siever	Detroit	1902	8-13	1.91
E. Walsh	Chicago	1910	18-20	1.27
S. Coveleski	Cleveland	1923	13-14	2.76

National League

Name	Team	Year	W-L	Era
D. Luque	Cincinnati	1925	16-18	2.63
D. Kolso	New York	1949	11-14	2.50
S. Miller	San Francisco	1958	6-9	2.47
N. Ryan	Houston	1987	8-16	2.76
J. Magrane	St. Louis	1988	5-9	2.18

Note that in the American League, L. Grove 1926, Philadelphia (1373), D. Donovan 1961, Washington (10-10) and D. (can't read) 1970 (10-10) all were ERA leaders.

Pitchers Who Won ERA Titles in Both Leagues

Hoyt Wilhelm was the first pitcher to cop the ERA title in both leagues. In 1952, he was primarily a relief pitcher, while in 1959 he became a starter. He is the only pitcher who can make that claim. Because of free league trading and the demise of free agency Randy Johnson and Pedro Martinez joined Wilhelm on the short list.

H. Wilhelm	New York	1952	2.43
	Baltimore	1959	2.19
R. Johnson	Seattle	1995	2.48
	Arizona	1999	2.48
	Arizona	2001	2.49
	Arizona	2002	2.32
P. Martinez	Montreal	1997	1.90
	Boston	1998	2.07
	Boston	1999	1.74
	Boston	2002	2.26
	Boston	2003	2.22

ERA Leader Two Different Teams Same League

This is also a short list of six members. Four times in the American League and twice in the National League has this scenario taken place.

American League

S. Coveleski	Cleveland	1923	2.76
	Washington	1925	2.84
L. Grove	Philadelphia	1926	2.51
	Philadelphia	1929	2.81
	Philadelphia	1930	2.54
	Philadelphia	1931	2.06
	Philadelphia	1932	2.84
	Boston	1935	2.70
	Boston	1936	2.81

110

| | | Boston 1938 | 3.07 |
| | | Boston 1939 | 2.54 |

| L. Tiant | Cleveland | 1968 | 1.60 |
| | Boston | 1972 | 1.91 |

R.Clemens	Boston	1986	2.48
	Boston	1990	1.93
	Boston	1991	2.62
	Boston	1992	2.41
	Toronto	1997	2.05
	Toronto	1998	2.65

National League

G. Alexander	Philadelphia	1915	1.22
	Philadelphia	1916	1.55
	Philadelphia	1917	1.83
	Chicago	1919	1.72
	Chicago	1920	1.91

| K. Brown | Florida | 1996 | 1.89 |
| | Los angles | 2000 | 2.58 |

A

Aaron, H   13, 56, 59
Adams   89, 97
Aguirre   96
Alexander29, 39, 40, 73, 85, 86, 87, 92, 93,
    98, 100, 103 110,
Alexander, D   68
Allison   12
Alomar   10
Alou, M   66
Altrock   39, 46, 48, 88
American League   3, 4, 5, 6, 7, 8, 9, 10, 11,
    12, 13, 15, 17, 18, 20, 22, 25, 26, 28, 29,
    31, 32, 37, 47, 51, 52, 53, 55, 56, 57, 59,
    60, 61, 63, 65, 66, 68, 69, 70, 71, 72, 74,
    75, 76, 77, 78, 79, 80, 81, 82, 83, 84, 85,
    86, 87, 88, 89, 90, 91, 93, 94, 95, 96,
    101, 102, 104, 105, 106, 108, 109, 110,
    111, 112, 113, 114
Ames   22
Anson   14
Appling, L   72
Armas   12
Astacio, P   35
Aurila, R   9, 11, 15, 72, 75
Avery, S   35

B

B. White   73
Babe Ruth   15, 17, 55, 57, 58, 62, 68
Bagby   21, 46, 47, 84
Bagwell, J   57, 60
Bahnsen, S   27, 35
Baker, F   18
Band Box   91
Banks, E   14, 15, 17, 73, 74, 83,
Bannister   48
Barker, L   32, 33
Barnes, J   22, 98
Baseball Hall of Fame   1
Bayne   89
Bell, B   66, 91
Belle, A   53, 57, 61, 62, 66, 67
Bench, J   76, 83
Benton   40, 41, 90, 97, 98
Benz   48, 95

Berenguer, J   48
Bernhard   44, 88
Berra, Y   16, 18
Bevens   95
Billingham, J   35, 47
Bishop, M   67
Blaeholder   29
Blankenship   33
Blue   22, 107, 108
Boddicker, M   48
Bonds, Barry 15, 17, 39, 53, 56, 57, 58, 59,,
    62, 64, 68, 69
Borbon, P   35
Boston Braves   73
Bosio   48
Boswell, D   23
Bottomley, J   55
Boudreau, L   9, 51, 53, 72
Bouton   91, 92
Bowman, J   27
Bradley, T   23
Bresnahan   18
Brett, G   55
Broberg   92
Brock, L   66, 81
Brown, K   25, 96, 97, 110
Buckner, B   66, 69
Buffalo   39, 93, 100, 101
Buhl, B   29
Buehle, M   40
Buhner, J   67, 72
Bunning   24, 104
Burchell   94
Burdette, L   29, 43
Burnett, A   34
Burtschy, M   32, 33
Busby   92
Bush,E   51
Bush, J   27

C

Caldwell, R   21
Campanella   16, 68, 72, 76, 83,
Campaneris   75
Candiotti   48
Carleton, T   28, 87
Carlton, S   24, 30, 99, 103 107, 108,
Carpenter, C   40

Carter, G 76
Cey 16
Chance, D 23, 86, 91
Chapman 51, 71
Chapman, B 67
Chase, H 88
Chech 89
Chesbro 22, 23, 27, 38, 84, 89
Chicago Whales 93
Cicotte 21, 33, 46, 89
Clauss 95
Clemens 24, 34, 96, 97, 99, 102, 110
Clement, M 25
Clemente 14, 18
Coakley 21, 46, 92
Cochrane, M 51, 67
Cobb 12, 14, 53, 55
Coleman, J 23, 43, 96
Collins, J 18
Collins, E 33, 51, 84, 85
Collins, R 79, 80, 81,
Combs 18
Cone 25, 104,
Coombs 38, 87, 90, 91
Coombs, E 67, 87, 89
Coombs, J 84, 85, 86, 89
Cooper, C 68
Cooper, M 32, 34, 35 39, 87, 94,
Cooper, W 15, 17, 28, 73
Cora, J 67
Corcoran, L 35, 36, 37, 38
Coveleski 21, 47, 108, 109
Craig, R 27
Cramer, D 70
Crandall, D 22
Crawford, J 54, 70
Crawford, S 65
Cronin, Jack 26
Cronin, Joe 16, 18
Crosetti, F 67
Crowder, A 29 33
Cubs 3, 4, 12, 14, 16, 17, 28, 29, 32, 37, 57, 65, 92, 93
Cuellar 21, 22
Currie 89
Cuyler, K 13, 60, 61, 65, 68, 73
Cy Young 18, 27, 90, 92, 93

Dale 98
Daniels 96
Darling, R 35
Daulton, D 76
Davenport, D 22, 46, 88, 96, 101
Dauss 30
Davis, T 63, 67
Dean, D 19, 85
Dean, P 40
Delahanty, E 54, 55
Dietrich 49, 95
Dickey 18
Dierker 24, 47, 95,
DiMaggio, D 67
DiMaggio, J 12, 15, 16, 18, 59, 60, 62, 65, 67, 71
Dinneen 21, 38, 46,
Dobson, P 22
Dodgers 4, 49, 71, 92
Doerr, B 9, 10, 11, 16, 18, 67, 71
Donahue, R 22
Donohue, P 22
Donovan, B 21
Dorner 26
Douglas, P 29
Downing 92
Dropo, W 67, 72
Drysdale 24, 26, 95
Duggleby 20, 22
Durham, L 88
Durham, R 67, 72, 92

D

Dahlen, B 73

E

Eckersley 35
Erksine 35
Earnshaw 21
Eason 26
English, W 60, 61, 64, 65, 69
Esper 46
Evans 12

F

Faber 21, 46, 84
Falkenberg 25, 96
Fanwell 94
Fassero 25

Feller   19, 21, 25, 86, 91, 98, 101, 102, 106, 107,

Ferguson, C   26
Fernandez, S   25
Fielder, C   55
Figueroa   92
Fillingim   27, 29
Fisk   18
Flanagan, M   33
Flood, C   69
Foley   36, 37
Ford, W   18, 30, 33
Forsch, B   35
Foster, G   56
Fox,   67, 68, 71, 73, 101
Foxx, J   16, 18, 53, 56, 57, 58, 59, 60, 62, 63, 65, 67, 69, 71,, 77,
Franco, J   68, 73
Fraser, C   26, 97
Freeman, B   65, 70
French, L   28
Frisch, F   18, 78, 80, 81,
Fryman, W   95
Furillo   16

G

Galarraga, A   63
Galehouse   49, 95, 96
Garcia, M   21
Garciaparra   72, 75
Garr, R   66, 70
Gaston, M   27
Gehrig   13, 16, 18, 53, 56, 57, 58, 59, 60, 62, 63, 65, 66, 67, 71
Gehringer, C   9, 54, 60, 67, 68, 71, 73
Giants   4, 13, 14, 16, 17, 19, 29, 37, 40, 70, 83, 92, 98
Gibson, B   24, 33, 43, 47, 87, 92, 94, 95,
Gilliam, J   67
Glade   27, 47, 88, 93
Glavine, T   30, 32 35,
Goldsmith, F   35, 36, 37
Gomez, L   13, 18, 19
Gonzalez, J   61, 62
Gooden, D   24, 25, 88
Gordon, J   67
Gordon, T   10,18, 34,
Gonzalez, L   53, 58, 59
Goslin, G   67
Gossage   18

Grant, M   47
Gray, S   29
Greenberg, H   54, 62, 67, 68, 71
Griffey, K. Jr   67
Griffin, T   24
Grimes, B   18, 19, 39
Grimsley, J   41
Griner   26, 97
Groat, D   70, 72, 73
Groom, B   27, 28, 46, 89
Grove, R   21, 49, 84, 98, 102, 109
Gubicza   48
Guidry   33
Gullet   35
Gura   33

H

Hack Wilson   6, 14, 16, 68
Haefner   33, 95, 96
Haines, J   19, 29, 88, 98
Hall   12
Hamilton, B   54, 55
Harang, A   40
Hargrave, E   76
Harmon, B   26
Harris   27,
Harris   27, 39, 40, 47, 48, 49, 93, 96
Hartnett   15, 17
Hass, M   67
Hayes, F   86, 96
Haynes   95, 96
Hearn, J   28
Heath, J   55
Heilmann   12
Heinrich, T   67
Helton, T   53, 58, 59, 60
Herma, B   59
Hershiser   35
Hess   21
High, A   51
Hodges, G   16, 68
Hodnett   38
Hoffman   93
Hollocher, C   51, 74, 75
Holmes, T   51
Holtzman, K   22
Hooper   18
Hollocher   53, 79, 80
Hornsby 15, 17, 50, 53, 55, 57, 59, 60, 62, 63, 67, 70, 71, 76, 81, 82,

114

Howell, H	27
Hough, C	34
Hoyt	18, 19
Hubbell	18, 30, 87, 94
Hudson, T	34, 40, 41
Hughes	21
Humphries	97
Hundley, T	83
Hunt	31, 94
Hunter, J	22, 33

I

Irv Young	26

J

Jackson, A	27
Jackson, J	70
Jackson, R	18
Jackson, T	17, 18
Jacobson, B	27, 68, 88, 89
James	33
Jansen, L	28
Jenkins, F	104
Jensen	16
Jeter, D	16, 75
Johnson, D	82
Johnson, H	78, 79
Johnson, K	101
Johnson, R	25, 35, 84, 86, 98, 100, 101 104,, 106, 108, 109
Johnson, Roy	68
Johnson, W	27, 84, 86, 90, 98, 102, 107,
Jones, A	12
Jones, C	12, 79
Jones, O	26
Jones, S	33
Joss	21, 46, 48, 89, 94

K

Kaat	23, 33, 92
Kaline	14
Kantlehner	98
Keating	95
Keefe	45
Keeler, W	71

Keister, B	54
Keller, C	12, 67
Kennedy	47, 96
Kent	15
Kerr	21
Keupper	28
Kile	25
Killebrew	12
Killen	45
Killian	21, 26, 27, 46, 48, 88,
King, C	28
Kingman, B	26
Kitson	47, 84, 88,
Klein, C	6, 50, 52, 53, 59, 60, 63, 64, 67, 69,
Koch, B	34, 36
Koch	35, 41, 96
Koosman	25
Koufax, S	24, 26, 87, 94, 106, 108
Kremer, R	28
Kuenn, H	75

L

LaJoie, N	70, 76, 77,
Lake, J	27, 94
Lamabe	96
Lary, L	67
Lazzeri	16
Leach, F	51
Lee, B	28
Lee, C	67
Leever	34
Leiber, H	69
Lemon, B	19, 21, 86, 91
Leverenz	95
Lidle, C	40, 41
Lindaman, V	26
Lindstrom	17, 18
Lolich	23, 30, 33, 107
Lombardi, E	76
Lonborg, J	32, 35
Lopez, A	18
Lopez, J	83
Luque	22, 29

M

Maddox, N	32, 34, 92
Maglie	28

Magrane, J	108
Malzone	16
Mantle	16, 18, 57, 78, 79, 80, 81, 85
Manush, H	70
Marchildon	96
Marqard	22
Marichal	23, 24, 30, 87, 93, 95,
Maroth	26
Martinez, E	67
Martinez, P	25, 105, 107, 108, 109
Martinez	72
Mathews	13
Mathewson	18, 20, 22, 30, 34, 85, 86, 87,
	92, 93, 99, 103, 107
Matlock	24, 35
Mattern, A	26
Mauer, J	76
May	42
Mays	13, 15, 17, 18
Mays, C	51
Mays, W	55, 56
Mazeroski	18
McAndrew, J	95
McCaskill	24
McConnell	95
McDowell, S	23, 25, 99, 107, 108,
McDowell, R	35
McGee, W	44, 79, 80
McGinnity	19, 22, 34, 85, 101, 103
McGregor, S	34, 48
McGriff, F	14, 65, 70
McGwire, M	57, 58, 64, 65
McInnis, S	50
McIntire, H	26
McLain, D	84, 89
McNally	21, 22
McQuillan	89
Meadows, L	29, 41, 97, 98
Medwick	59, 61, 63, 66, 67
Messersmith	35, 105
Mets	82, 92
Miller, W	88
Millwood, K	34, 35
Mitchell, C	29
Mitchell, D	50, 51
Mize, J	15, 17, 77
Molitor, P	68, 70, 76
Montanez, W	81
Moore, J	66, 69
Moore, M	33, 34, 70, 73
Morgan	33
Morris, J	34
Morrison, J	29
Moseley	25, 39
Mueller, B	78
Mueller, D	50, 51
Mulder, M	40, 41
Mullin, G	21, 26, 27, 28, 30, 48
Murray, E	56, 79, 84
Musial, S	53, 56, 57, 59
Mussina	24
Myers, E	27

N

Nagy	34
Naylor	27
Nehf	22
Newsom	33, 48
Newhouser	19, 102
Nettles	16
New York Giants	70
New York Highlanders	90
New York Mets	82
New York Yankees	3, 4, 8, 13, 14, 17, 31,
	53, 71
Newhouser, H	30, 33
Newsom	33
Nichols	31, 42
Niekro, J	48, 96
Niekro, P	26, 30, 95
Nomo, H	105
Nuxhall, J	101

O

O'Doul	50, 52, 60, 68, 69, 71
Oeschger	29
Oliver, D	35
Oliver, A	69
Ordonez, M	67
Orosco, J	96
Orth	22, 23, 27, 38, 39, 42, 89
Osteen, C	48
Ott	13, 14, 15, 17, 18, 63, 67

P

Padilla	35
Paige	19

116

Palmeiro, R	68
Palmer, J	20, 21, 22, 86, 92, 96
Park	25
Pastorius	26, 92
Patten, C	27, 40, 46, 89
Pattin	92
Pendleton, T	78, 79, 80, 81,
Pennock	18, 19
Perritt	39, 40, 41, 97
Perry, G	24, 33, 105
Perry, S	27
Perzanowski	97
Pesky, J	67, 75
Petrocelli, R	82
Pettitte	30
Pfeffer, P	26
Philadelphia A	3, 19, 31, 32, 48, 71, 90
Piazza, M	83
Pipgras, G	32, 33
Pirates	7, 14, 17, 28, 29, 31, 77
Pittinger	26
Plank, E	21, 22, 23, 38, 46, 90
Podres	35, 48
Pole	92
Posey, B	76
Powell	93
Prudhomme	33

Q

Quinn	33

R

Radbourn, C	36, 38
Radcliff, R	71
Radke	41
Ragan	41, 98
Raines, T	79
Ramirez, H	73
Ramirez, M	62, 66
Reese, P	68
Regan	96
Reisling	94
Reyes, J	73, 79, 80
Reynolds, S	25
Rhoads	21
Rice	12, 16
Rice, J	59
Rice, S	51

Richard, J	107
Ripken, C	56
Rixey	22, 39
Rizzuto	18
Robinson, J	16, 67
Roberts, R	30, 43, 103
Rodriguez	8, 10, 42, 72, 77, 78, 79, 80, 87
Rodriguez, A	62, 67, 72, 73, 74, 75, 82, 83,
Rogell, B	9, 67
Rolfe, R	67
Rose, P	71, 78, 79, 80, 101,
Roush, E	51
Rucker	40, 97
Rudolph	41, 97, 98
Ruelbach	34, 93, 96
Ruffing	18, 19,30,
Russell, J	27
Russell	33
Ruth	16, 18, 53, 55, 56,
57, 58, 59, 60, 61, 63, 64, 65, 67, 77	
Ryan, N	23, 24, 96, 97, 98, 100,
105, 106, 108,	

S

Saberhagen, B	48
Sadecki, R	43, 48,
Sallee	39, 41, 92
Sandberg, R	82
Santo	15, 17
Savage	95
Sax, S	70
Schilling	25, 35, 107,108
Schneider	40, 97, 98
Schoendienst	80, 81,
Schulte, F	55
Score, H	21
Scott, J	27
Scott, M	107
Seaver	24, 25 100,
Segui, D	84
Selee, F	31
Senators	73, 90
Severeid, H	50
Sewell, J	18, 51, 52, 54, 67
Shea	92
Sheckard, J	31
Sheffield	12
Shore	96
Short, C	24

Shulz   33, 90
Shupp   39
Sierra, R   68, 79, 80, 81,
Simmons, A   45, 50, 57, 58, 60, 62, 63, 66,
    67, 70, 76, 99
Singer, B   23, 24, 106
Sisler, G   49, 51, 68, 69, 74
Smith, Bob   96
Smith, Eddie   34, 48, 50
Smith, Elmer   44
Smith, F   21
Smith, J   46
Smith, P   41, 85
Smith, Reggie   81
Smith, Sherry   96
Smoltz, J   30
Snider, D   16, 67
Sosa   15, 17, 53, 57, 58, 59, 62, 63, 64, 65,
    69
Spahn   26, 29, 30, 43, 101, 102,
Sparks   89
Speaker   18, 50, 51, 70
Spence, S   54
St. Louis Browns   19, 28, 51, 73
St. Louis Terriers   93
Staley   31, 45
Stargell   18
Steele   41, 89
Stephens, V   9, 11, 61, 67, 72, 73, 77, 82,
    83,,
Stewart, D   34
Stivetts   31, 45
Stock, M   70, 71
Sudhoff   27
Summa, H   51
Sutton, D   24, 35, 48,
Suzuki, I   50
Swindell, G   48

T

Talbot   96
Tanana   23, 24, 92
Tannehill   21, 39, 46, 93
Taylor, D   22
Taylor, J   22
Ted Williams   15, 17, 58, 63, 66, 68
Teixeira, M   79
Tejada, M   8, 62, 73
Templeton   84
Terry, B   6, 18, 49, 50, 69

Terry, R   33
Tesreau   22, 39
Thomas,F   34, 57, 67
Thompson   73, 95, 96
Thompson, F   69
Thompson, S   54, 55
Thormahlen   33
Tiant   23, 92, 110
Tobin, J   68
Toney, F   22, 98
Torrez, M   33
Townsend, J   27
Trammell   11, 12
Travis, C   75
Traynor   18, 51
Triple Crown   13, 81
Trosky, H   59, 62, 67
Troy   37, 38, 89
Tudor, J   88, 96
Twins   42, 75

V

Valentin, J   67
Vance   19, 99
Vaughan, A   73
Veach   12
Velarde   85, 86
Verban, E   51
Vernon, M   54
Viola, F   48
Vosmik, J   70

W

Waddell   23, 46, 88, 89 99, 106, 107
Wagner   14, 18, 54, 55, 58, 72, 73, 74, 75,
    77,
Walberg, G   21
Walker, G   16, 54, 68
Walker, L   57, 59
Walters, B   27
Waner, L   18, 51
Waner, P   14, 18
Walsh, E   21, 38, 39, 84, 85,89, 108
Ward   36,
Warhop   94
Warneke   28, 34, 40, 94
Washington Senators   73
Wegman, B   34, 48,

118

Weimer	22
Westbrook, J	40
White, B	69
White, D	21
White Sox	37, 50, 90, 91
Whitney, J	28
Whitney, P	69
Wicker	22
Wilhelm	26, 109
Williams, Bernie	78
Williams, Billy	14, 15, 17
Williams, C	21
Williams, J	54
Williams, K	62
Williams	67
Williams, S	24
Williams, T	16, 18, 56, 57, 60, 61, 64
Willis, V	26
Wills, M	66, 70
Wilson, D	24, 54
Wilson, H	15, 17, 57, 59, 63, 65, 69
Wilson, W	78, 80
Winfield, D	56
Witt, B	24
Witt, M	24

Wood, J	33, 84, 85, 86, 90
Wood, K	25
Wood, W	23, 27
World Series	4, 18, 30, 52, 90
Wright	16
Wynn, E	19, 21

Y

Yde	28
Yerkes	33
Young, C	18, 21 27, 38, 39, 46, 84, 85, 87, 88, 89, 92, 103
Young, I	26
Youngs	18
Yount, R	68, 72, 74

Z

Zimmerman, H	77, 82
Zito, B	40 41

119

Frank MacKay's career in entertainment and politics spans four decades. In 1985, at the age of 18, he published his first music publication, "Network", with his brother, Gordon. Soon after, it became a hit among music business insiders, musicians and their fans. Throughout the next ten years, MacKay built a significant following in the music industry as a band and club promoter, managing entertainers such as Criss Angel and CJ Ramone. He also launched a small chain of nightclubs on Long Island, New York. MacKay was also interested in politics at a young age, and in 1992 he became engaged in Ross Perot's run for the United States presidency. In the year 2000, MacKay decided to run for State Chairman of the Independence Party of New York. He won the election, and became the youngest State Chairman of a political party in New York State history. He has since been re-elected to that position eight consecutive times. The Independence Party of New York presently has more than 450,000 members and is the fastest growing third party political organization in the nation. It is the largest third party in the history of the United States. In 2007, MacKay was also elected National Chair of the Independence Party of America. Frank hosts a daily talk show on LI News Radio, as well as a nationally syndicated show.

Gordon MacKay is a financial adviser based in the Boston area. This is Gordon's second book in collaboration with his brother Frank. Throughout his successful career as a manager and agent, he has guided the careers of entertainment and sports stars including Evel Knievel, Eddie Money, the Flying Wallendas, Criss Angel and more. Gordon lives in New England with his wife Marybeth and their son Justin.